The Irish Concertina

A TUTOR FOR THE ANGLO CONCERTINA IN THE IRISH STYLE

Devised & written by Mick Bramich

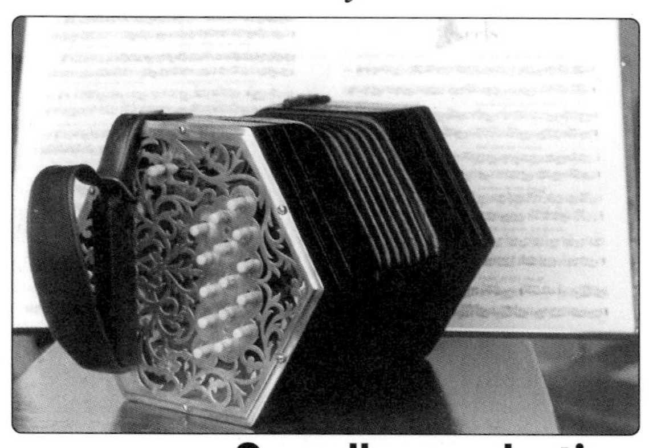

A mally production

The Irish Concertina

Recording

A soundtrack (DMPCD9601) has been produced to complement this tutor book; it contains extracts from each chapter and some of the tunes from *Appendix one*...it should be available from wherever you purchased this book but if you have any difficulty obtaining the soundtrack, please contact the publishers.

The Irish Concertina **A Tutor for the Anglo Concertina in the Irish Style by Mick Bramich**

ISBN 1 899512 25 X

A catalogue in print record for this title is available from the British Library

Devised and written by Mick Bramich
Cover photograph of Mick Bramich by Linda Bramich
All other photographs by Mick Bramich unless otherwise stated
Thanks to Bruce M Baillie for help with the Celtic illustrations

First printed in England 1996. Re-printed 2000 & 2005 by Fretwell Print and Design, Keighley

Produced and published by mally.com
3 East View, Moorside, Cleckheaton, West Yorkshire, BD19 6LD
Telephone +44 (0)1274 876388 facsimile +44 (0)1274 865208
Email mally@mally.com Web http://www.mally.com

A mally production

Contents

Linda Branich

A session at Donnelly's, Barna, County Galway

On the left is Tim Lyons, a fine singer and box player and a great teacher. He has had a major influence on the music that I play and I hold him responsible!

The Irish Concertina

Index of tunes

Alternative titles are shown in *italics*

INTRODUCTION

It has long been a source of enquiry for me, that the Anglo concertina seems to have fallen into the hands of people who cannot and, indeed, will not acknowledge the instrument's full potential. This is not a quote from some long forgotten authority but simply a comment upon the state of playing as I see it in my travels around the music scene in England. Apart from a small handful of well respected mentors of the 'English' style (William Kimber to name but one and his influence obviously in terminal decline), I see and hear no-one implementing a more melodic method than the rather tired and well-worn 'up and down the rows' system.

There has been a trend in recent years to devise key structures for the instrument which are 'easy' for the player as opposed to sticking to what you have and utilising the chromatic possibilities of the object which is in your hands. I refer mainly to the big reed concertinas in the keys of D and G which have found favour amongst many band players during the last fifteen years or so. There are some very fine examples of these instruments made by modern craftsmen and I do not wish anything in this paragraph to be seen as derogatory but the fact exists that by making these custom boxes, the older skills attached to playing instruments in the C and G layout have largely been forgotten.

This is merely sucking up to the phenomenal success accorded to the melodeon and its progeny which have become richly endowed with carvings and gold leaf in very recent times. Take a Hohner 'pokerwork' model to a session and wait for the hum of disapproval to become evident before your, by now, tame excuse that "I prefer the heavier action and..." whatever-comes-into-your-head-next reply to the wealthy owners of these *Cadillacs* of the morris and band scene!

The idea that using a C and G Anglo concertina is difficult is a myth and it is my pleasant duty to inform you that there is nothing sacred or mysterious in the style of playing that is given the rough and possibly inaccurate appellation 'Irish'. It is a system, plain and simple. Just as our forebears nourished systems on their spinets, lutes and citterns, so the traditional players of the Anglo have adopted means by which to exploit the little box of tricks and make it appear that their genius is something that mere mortals cannot strive to achieve. By the application of dedication and a thorough understanding of the layout of the buttons on your three-row Anglo, you can make the beast sing as never before...trust me!

It is not totally essential that you have to be able to read musical notation but it does help to show you why so many people are frightened by the notion of full blown melody playing in the keys that the tunes are written in. A fellow Anglo player who was a guest at a workshop that I attended a few years ago, had done his homework and duly presented a fistful of pieces suitable for most levels of attainment on the instrument. We began with a Playford dance tune written in the key of G major. To my horror, the workshop leader said that even though it was written in G (and had therefore been played in that key by generations of musicians from the seventeenth century onwards), we would play it in C as it would be 'easier'. At this point I decided that something had to be done about the ignorance attached to the playing of music on the humble Anglo in its correct key signature.

I had no formal tuition in musical theory or in concertina methodology. I will not be so bold as to say "It just came to me" because I would be a fraud but the method was arrived at independently and without having heard 'Irish' style playing prior to my discovery of the technique. It was pointed out to me by my late friend, Harry Boardman, that I played in the Irish style. Until that night in a Birmingham folk club, I was blissfully unaware of any pigeonholing or categorisation of the sound that I was making. So if I can 'stumble' upon the system, I am sure that with a little help, you can find your way into it by a more direct route and with some advice on the pitfalls and demons that you may encounter along the road to a broader understanding of the instrument and its possibilities.

Mick Bramich

Mick Bramich
April 1996

Choosing the Right Instrument

Thirty bone or metal buttons, fret-worked wooden or metal ends, five or six folds of reasonably thick and supple leather and you have the makings of a quality Anglo concertina. The test is to pick the thing up and feel how it fits and works for you. Therein lies one problem facing the would-be purchaser: *where do I get one?*

I have never bought a concertina by mail order but as long as there is an approval system in operation by the retailer then there should be no problems encountered. However, there is no substitute for having a rake of them on a table in front of you so that you can compare the qualities and deficiencies of a wide variety of makes and models. It costs a lot by post to get your hands on half a dozen possibles!

You may be fortunate enough to live close to a dealer or retailer (see *Appendix five*). If not, then it may be worth a telephone call to talk over the maybes and perhaps that can surround a particular model. A good alternative to all methods noted so far is a visit to a large folk festival where the major retailers are generally happy to let you squeeze your way through their shelves and give advice on certain points of etiquette such as "Don't drop that in the mud..." and so on.

A concertina playing workshop can also give good clues to the novice player and help to determine your course of action. After all, you may buy the confounded thing and then decide that it is not for you! You will ***not*** get what you paid for it when you ditch it. Most workshops will have people who are prepared to let you try their instruments out, under scrutiny of course; it could determine whether you proceed further or forget the whole issue and take up the comb and paper instead.

Specific Makes

Jeffries and Wheatstone models tend to be very air efficient and, when in good repair, may not need lots of attention paying to the air button. Jones and Lachenal instruments however, have a tendency to be a bit leaky and want more air availability to make them flow nicely. Many modern instruments in the upper price range are close to the old classics but some of the beginners' models on offer are only a short step from being an insult to the concertina family. In between the two major groups of instruments, i.e., the old and the modern, are the models made by the Crabb factory in London until quite recent times. They are often very plain but well made and difficult to come by second-hand. They are usually very bright in tone and can be found in various keys mainly in concert pitch (A = 440 hertz). In 1996, you would expect to pay anything from £300·00 for the lower end of the range to around £1,200·00 for a really good Jeffries. Crabb would be around the upper middle ground. Modern, quality copies will set you back about £1,900·00 to £3,000·00 or more for the very best.

Limits do exist and I know only too well that financial considerations are paramount in reaching any decision. I would urge you, if you do not already possess an instrument, to go for the most that you can afford. By doing this, you will be starting at an advantage not only because of the air problems mentioned earlier but also the whole playing action improves with every pound that you are prepared to spend.

Do not concern yourself with lashings of gold-leaf and heavily embossed leatherwork. This usually indicates that the bellows may be the originals and unless they are of the substantial construction, common in a Jeffries concertina, it may not be a blessing. Plain, black or dark brown bellows without decorative papers are perfectly adequate. Quality cannot be disguised by flash trimmings and accessories.

Likewise with the end-plates, raised metal or carved ebony may look nice but what does it sound like? These materials often impart harsh overtones which can be controlled but only by careful use of the air button.

Beware of sloppy rebuilds which leak; sticking buttons can be sorted out cheaply and ill-fitting pads are easily replaced; make sure that the thing is in tune. Concert pitch with A at 440 hertz is essential and, nowadays, quite the norm in the main market place. Obtaining one from uncle what's-'is-name's loft can create embarrassment when you turn up at your first session with A at 415 or some other obscure French orchestral pitch which was fashionable in 1891—and then only for a year! Re-tuning is costly and time consuming so do heed this advice.

The act of buying and selling concertinas should be a pleasurable one so, go ahead and start enjoying yourself!

A top class Jeffries G/C from around 1890

Castle near Kinvara on Galway Bay

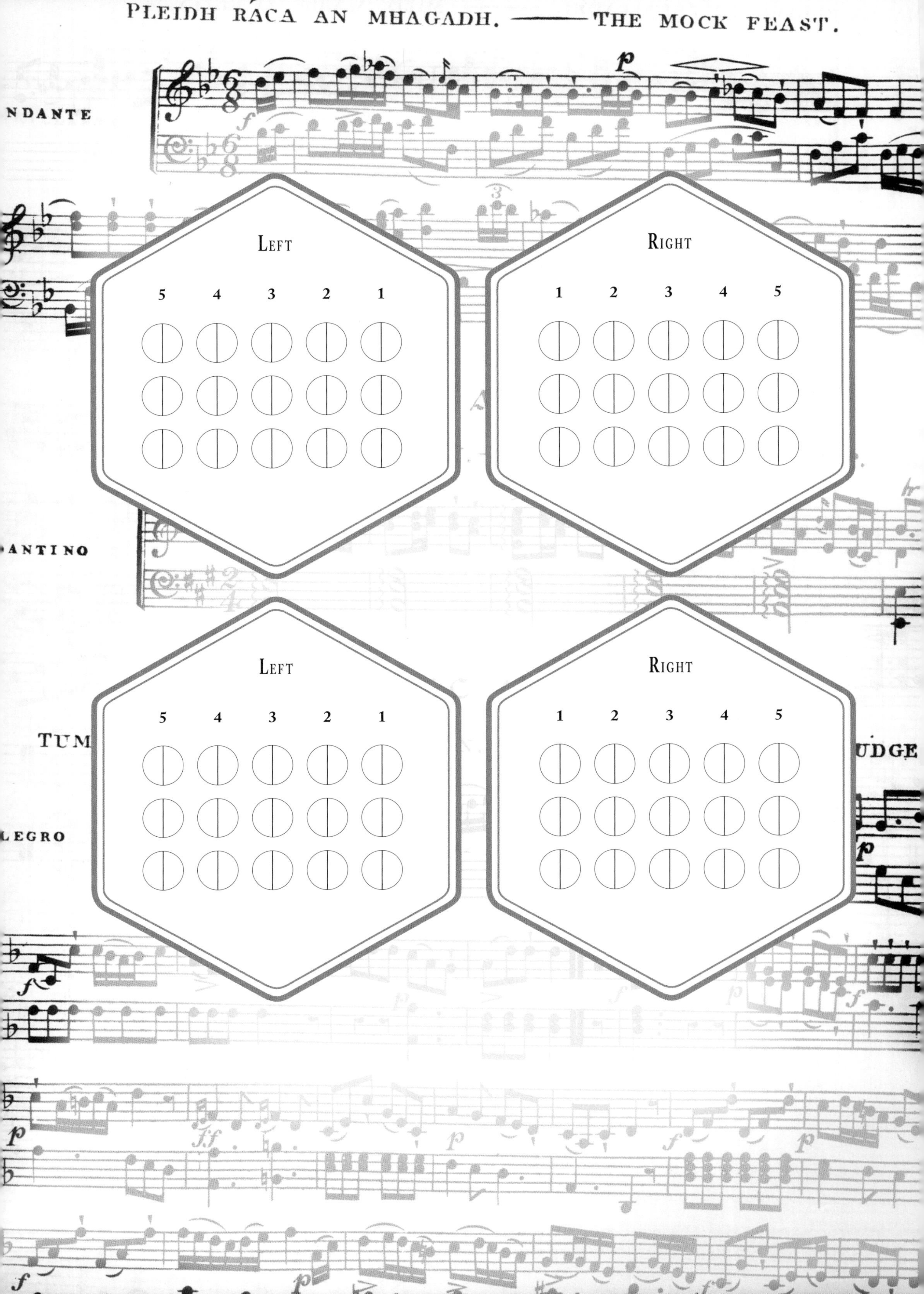
PLEIDH RACA AN MHAGADH. —— THE MOCK FEAST.
NDANTE
ANTINO
TUM
UDGE
LEGRO
Left
5 4 3 2 1
Right
1 2 3 4 5
Left
5 4 3 2 1
Right
1 2 3 4 5

About the Anglo concertina

If you possess a three-row Anglo in G and C then read on. The system analysed in this tutor will fit any three-row instrument but the keys available will vary with the particular tuning of your box. For example, I have a very nice Jeffries in F and B flat and consequently, all the key possibilities will be one whole tone lower than on a G and C model. A chart of possible keys relating to a range of tunings is shown in *Appendix two.*

A belief held by many people is that the Anglo is only any good for playing tunes an octave above the written score. This rumour has to be quashed. The temptation to push and pull up and down the diatonic rows is the first area to be tackled and this series of lessons is an attempt to get you to re-examine the instrument. The adage about old dogs and new tricks springs to mind but the mould can be broken.

The layout of your instrument

I wonder how many of you have taken the time to draw a plan of the ends of your Anglo showing which button does what and the direction of the air flow involved? It may sound like teaching your grandmother etc., but it is a valuable exercise and an essential one if you wish to go any further with the method on offer. Opposite are two blank layouts for you; use a pencil until you're confident you have it right. As a suggestion, use the left-hand half of each button for the press notes, the right-hand side for the draw notes.

Figure 1 below shows the simple but effective system with coded messages covering direction, note names, etc used throughout this book. A black square is a ***PUSH*** and a white square a ***PULL***. Remember, ***BLACK*** and ***WHITE***, ***PUSH*** and ***PULL***. Variations on this layout are likely depending upon the make, age and state of originality of your instrument. If it differs considerably, then I would suspect that the concertina has been laid out to suit a player with another system of playing. Reeds can be juggled around in their pans to bring notes into the configuration shown without great expense or use of time.

Air buttons are a source of concern to me. I arrived at the concertina via a circuitous route which involved B/C button accordeons, D/G melodeons and the basic two row, diatonic Anglo. The air button or lever on the accordeon and melodeon is on the left-hand side, assuming that you are right-handed. When changing to the concertina, it reverts to the right-hand and this can cause problems for the potential player. I was no exception to this clash of position and I could not get on with the right-hand air control; I still cannot to this day. If you suffer from this self-same inability to adapt, then there are ways of overcoming it.

The left-hand side often has a rogue button in the place corresponding to the right-hand air control. It may be a drone (often totally unrelated to any handy key on the instrument) or one of those quaint sound effect reeds common to examples from the heyday of the marriage between music hall performers and the Anglo. If so, then a little surgery can produce a ready-made left-hand air button. If you do not have this option available on your box, it can be set in place by a good maker or repairer at little cost and with no detrimental results to the quality of the machine.

Good advice would be to learn to use the right-hand button and if you are coming to the Anglo 'cold' with no prior knowledge of other bellowed instruments, then you are in a nice position to ignore this information altogether!

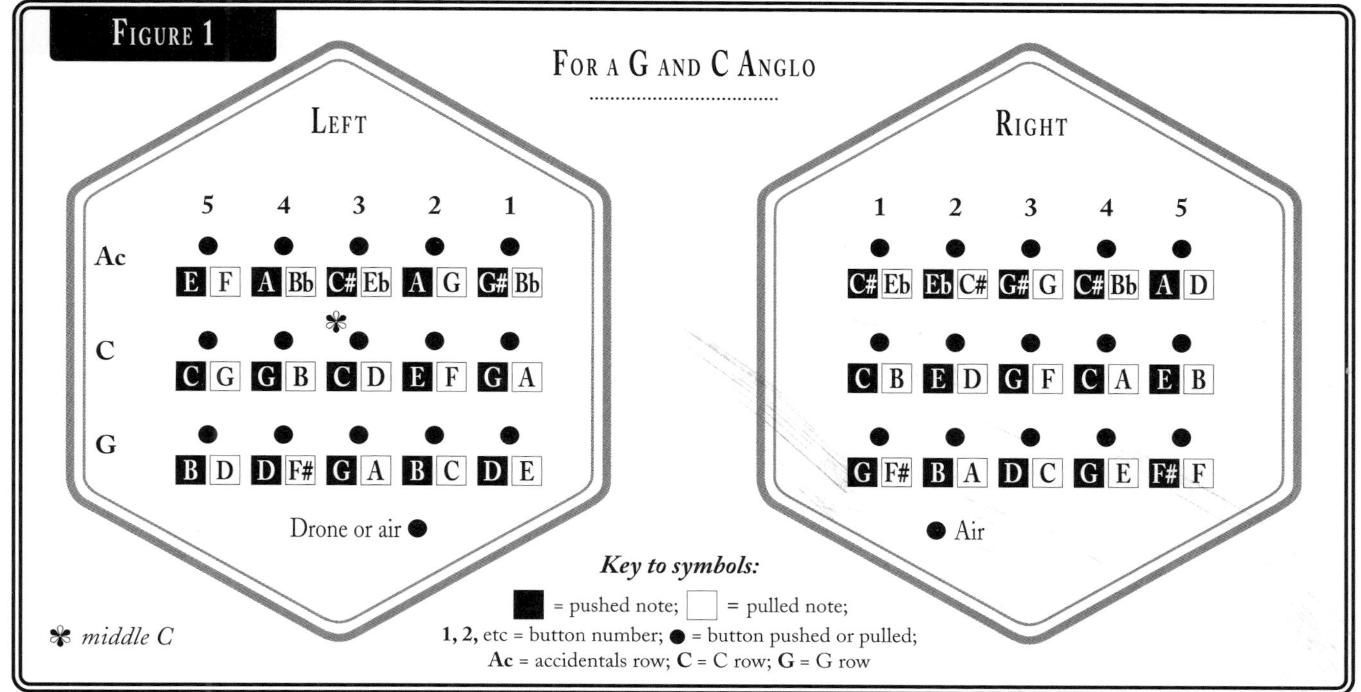

At this point, it would be wise to see just where the available notes on the instrument actually fit on the music stave. *Figure 2a,* below, starts with middle C, that is, the note which lies exactly mid-way between the treble and bass clef staves. The middle C on your box can be found on the pushed 3rd button of the left-hand C row.

The number represents the button and the letter the row on which the note is found. Remember, ■ is a pushed note and □ is pulled.

Figures 2a, b and *c* all represent notes from the key of C: don't worry just yet about the fact that you have to swap rows.

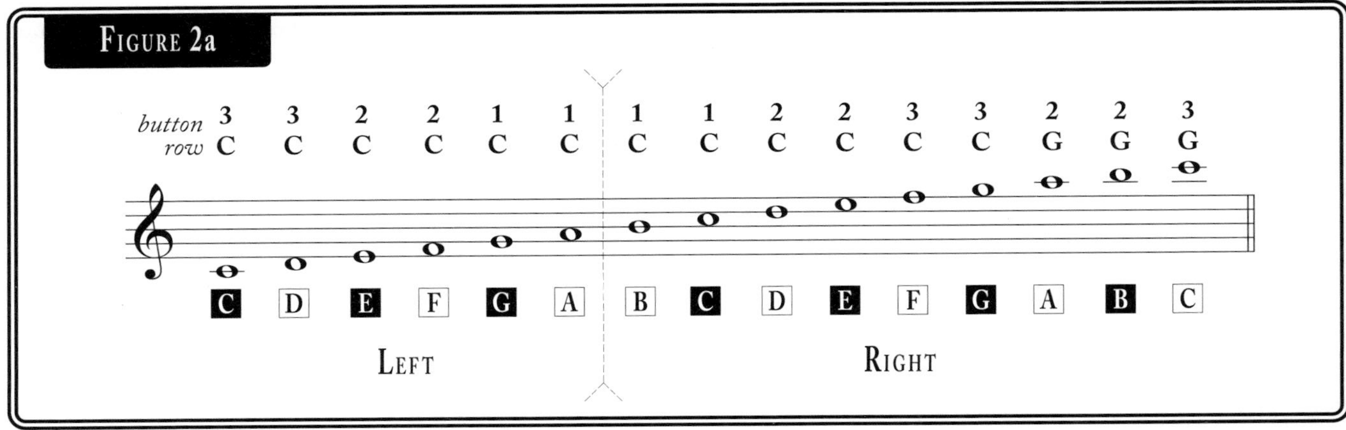

The notes go below middle C and should, in theory, be written on the bass clef as follows:

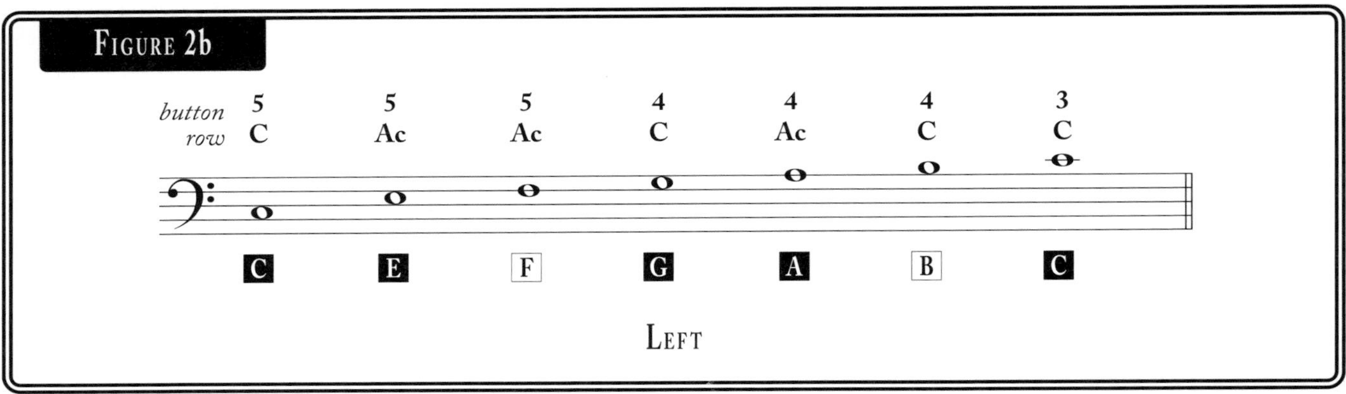

All the notes above G in the right hand are written on leger lines to show their position above the stave:

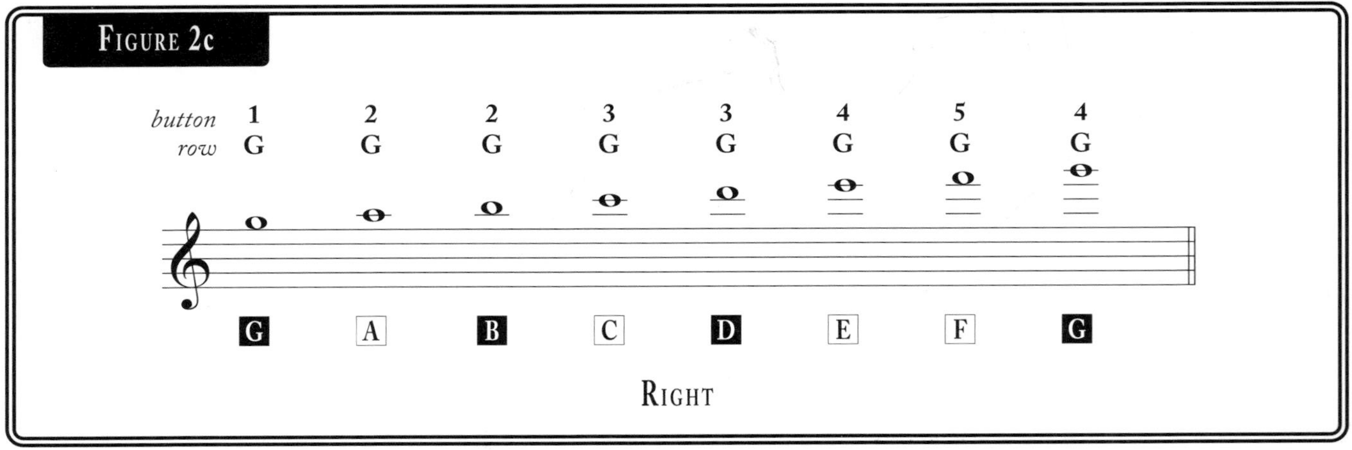

The key of G major

Having made the chart, we can now begin to look in more detail at the ways available to us for playing in different keys by applying the 'method'. I will assume that you have discovered the basics and know that pushing and pulling along the C row will produce the key of C major, interrupted by various strains of heavy breathing and rasping caused by ill-fitting valves or holed bellows! We can go straight for the next easiest key, that of G major but we are going to stay on the C row for the moment.

What makes G major different to C major? In traditional music terms, it is no more than the inclusion of F♯ and the need to start the scale in an alternative place on the row. The key of G commences on the left-hand side by pushing the topmost button on the C row. The simplest progression through the scale is done by next pulling the same button to get an A. By continuing to pull the air through and moving onto the first button on the right-hand side, you will find B. Push the same for C, pull the next button for D, then push for E and that's as far as you go along that row. By pulling the first right-hand button on the G row, you have found F♯. Push the same button to finish the scale on a G, one octave above your starting position.

Practise this scale for fifteen minutes. Try fitting a tune into the scale that is familiar to you; it does not have to be Irish for many French and English tunes sound well played by this method. The chart in *figure 3* below may help if you are finding diffculty with reading the text and playing the scale at the same time.

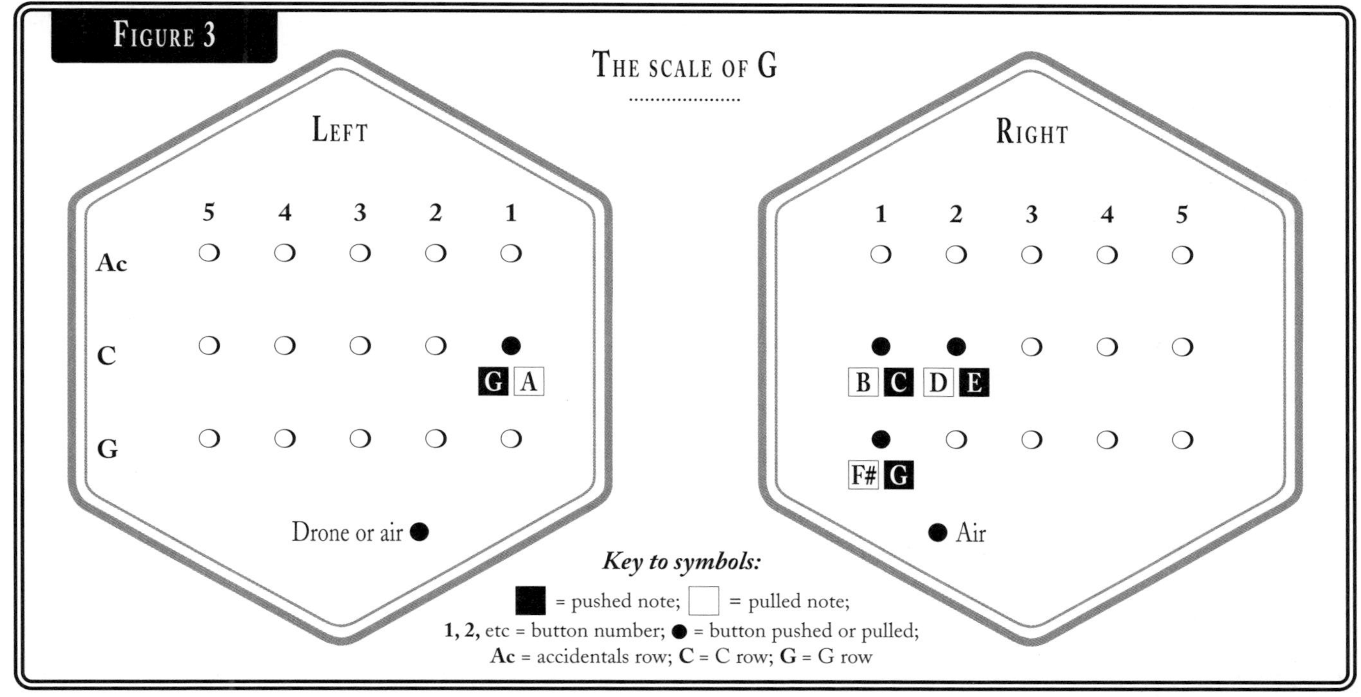

Extended scale of G

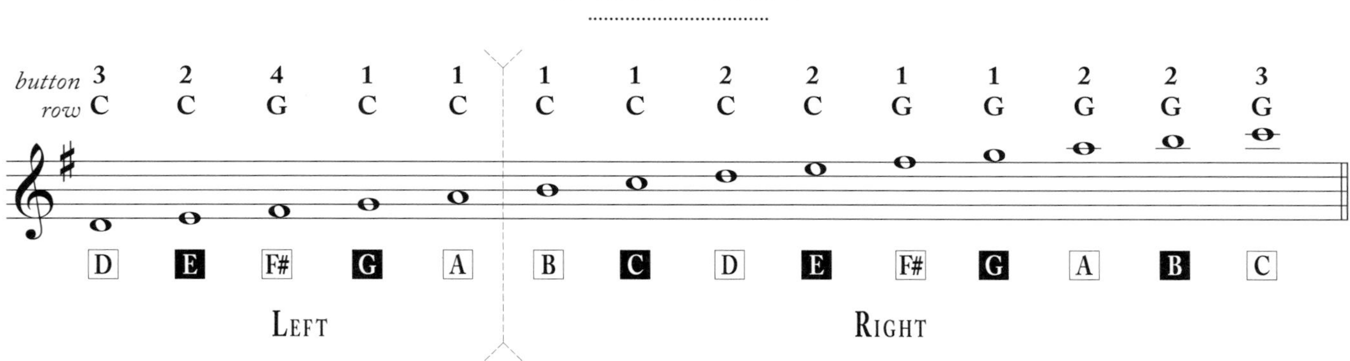

Do not forget, this system depends on you having a good knowledge of the direction of the bellows and the note that will consequently be produced. Therefore, even if the progression on the chart appears to be out of sequence, by changing the direction of the bellows you can bring the scale back into line.

Following are two examples of tunes which you can play using this first step. They are both within one octave and so should not create any real problems. Do not play them too fast as the method so far is still based on push and pull. More speed will be achieved when we move onto finding the scale of G by pulling the notes out of the box.

You will notice that the first tune, ***Cock o' the north,*** well known to most people, contains no F♯ notes. This will ease you into the system. ***The hullichan jig,*** another favourite at sessions and with dance bands, brings the F♯ on the right-hand G row in for the first time. This makes you cross onto the G row. The only tricky bit is in bar 12 where a rapid change in the direction of the bellows is called for. Remember to always play at a speed at which you can comfortably manage the hardest parts.

Notes within the key of G major will be encountered if you proceed beyond the first button on the right-hand side G row or go below the top button on the left-hand C row but diffculties will arise in the left hand because of the F♯. This left-hand side F♯ is the biggest obstacle to overcome if you want to go further with this technique. Its position on the end can only be described as awkward. After a lot of cursing and threatening to ditch the whole idea, it will suddenly click and you will be into another realm of style.

The fingers chosen to play these oddly placed notes must be thought about with care: they can affect the flow of a tune quite seriously. *Figures 4a* and *4b* show the progression down to D, far enough for many G tunes. Firstly, place the fingers of the left hand as shown in *figure 4a.* It is quite comfortable and logical on paper. By pushing or pulling you will achieve a dissonant chord which no sane player would wish to use in earnest. The little finger of the left hand must be trained to carry out the execution of F♯ at all times. By cracking this technique, you open up a whole range of other keys, both major and minor, all dependent on this simple action. Practise this four finger, left hand progression. Try it in both directions before moving onto the next stage.

The hullichan jig

Track 2

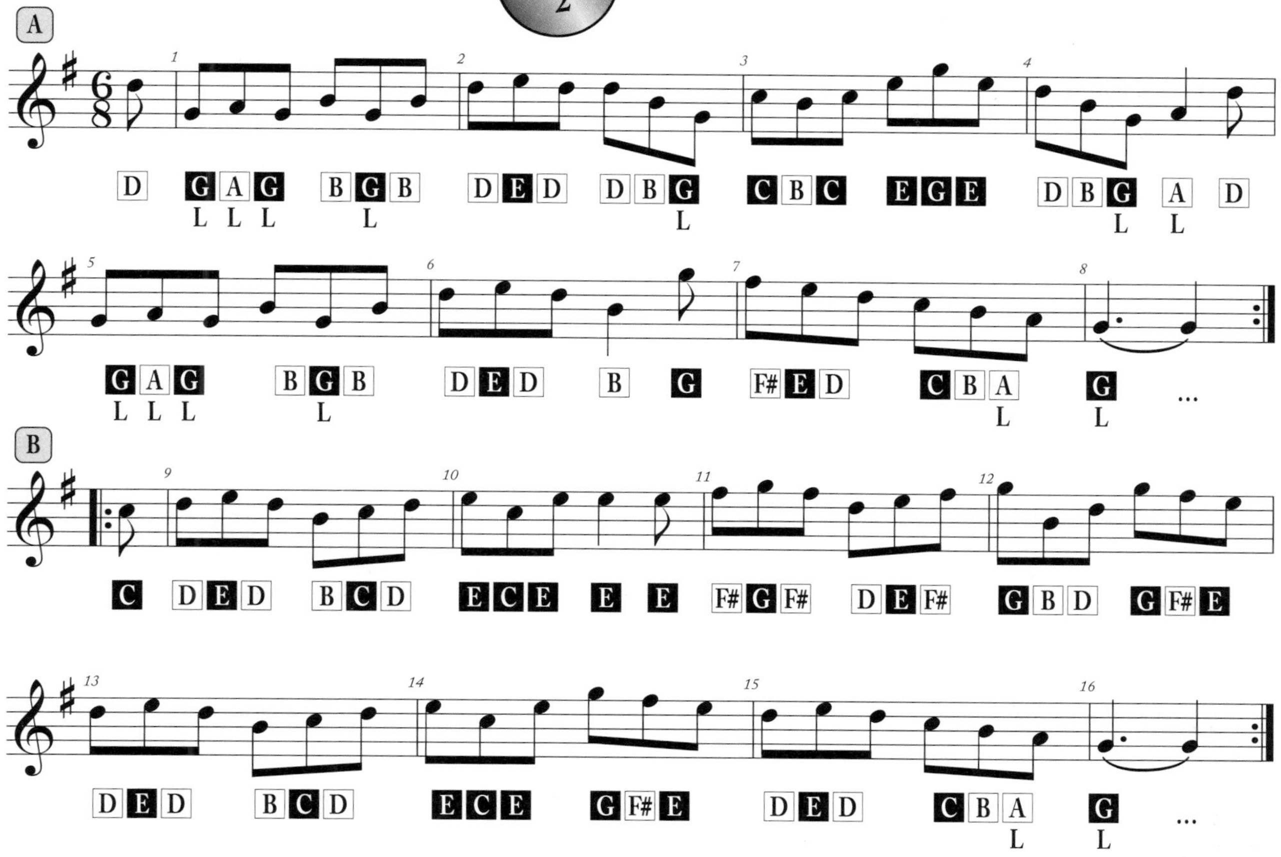

A
D GAG BGB DED DBG CBC EGE DBG A D
L L L L L L L
GAG BGB DED B G F#ED CBA G ...
L L L L L L
B
C DED BCD ECE E E F#GF# DEF# GBD GF#E
DED BCD ECE GF#E DED CBA G ...
L L

FIGURE 4a

positions

LEFT
5 4 3 2 1
Ac
C
3 2 1
G
4
Drone or air

FIGURE 4b

progression

LEFT
5 4 3 2 1
Ac
C
D E G
G
F#
Drone or air

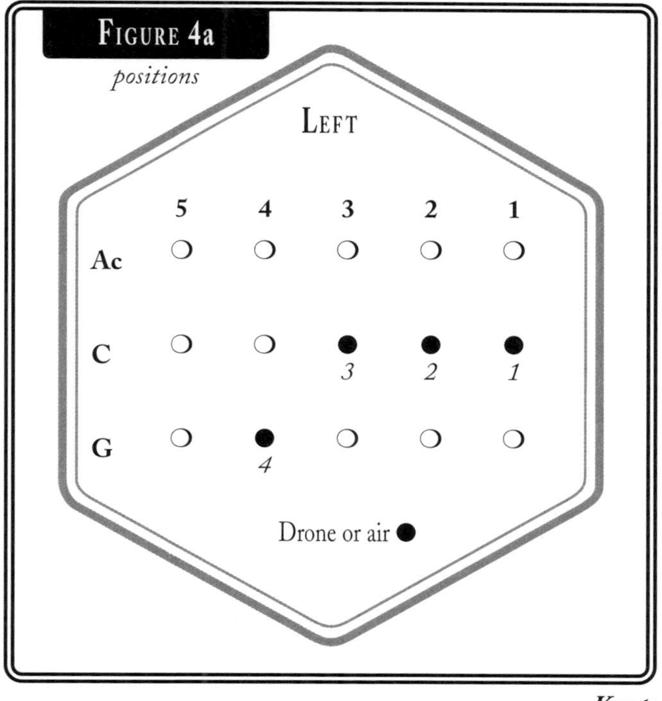

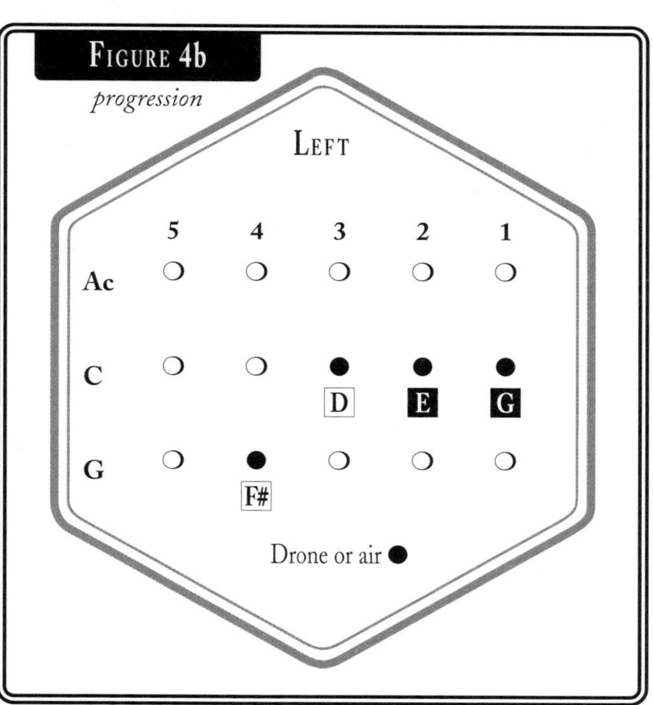

Key to symbols:

■ = pushed note; □ = pulled note;

1, 2, etc = button number; ● = button pushed or pulled;

1, 2, etc = finger

Ac = accidentals row; **C** = C row; **G** = G row

Here are two examples which take the melody below G and exploit the use of the little finger for producing F♯. Remember that on most instruments, there will be only one F♯ and one E in the correct register to complete the run successfully. Some larger format Anglos with another row of buttons nearer to the hand-straps may have duplicate F♯ and E notes but do not bank on it and anyway, you may need to play a basic three row, thirty button box at some point so you should know the technique.

Off to California, below, is a very good practise piece and well known into the bargain. The triplet notes may cause trouble at this stage so an alternative start is shown at the end of the tune. As you can see, much of the 'A' music is played by the left hand.

The second tune, shown opposite, ***Out on the ocean***, should feel comfortable by now. There are no major problems with it and again, it is an often-played and much-loved melody.

The *figures 5a* and *5b* opposite give the progression above the octave G on the right-hand side. C should be high enough for most purposes. Position the fingers as shown in *figure 5a* and try this exercise. Push the first button to achieve a G, pull the next button along the row for A, push that same button for B and pull the third for C. Practise this exercise until a fluid link is made between all the notes of the half scale. Practise the whole scale from the low D on the left-hand side C row to the top C on the right-hand side G row.

Much of ***The kesh jig*** (page 12) is played on the right hand side and B (pushed 2nd button on the G row) is as high as it goes. A session favourite, it can be heard on (for instance) early Boys of the Lough recordings from around 1973/4. ***The morning star*** (also page 12) is a reel from O'Neill's 'The Dance Music of Ireland: 1,001 Gems' but played slowly, it becomes a gentle little hornpipe. I think that it may have been the first reel that I ever learned.

Off to California

Track 3

A

D E F# G F# G B A G E D

L L L L L L R L L L

B

* Alternative to triplet

D F#

L L

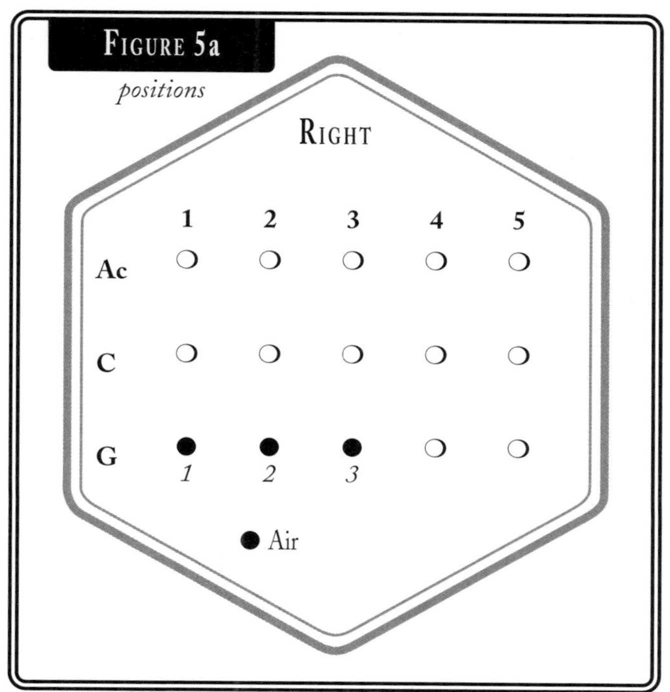

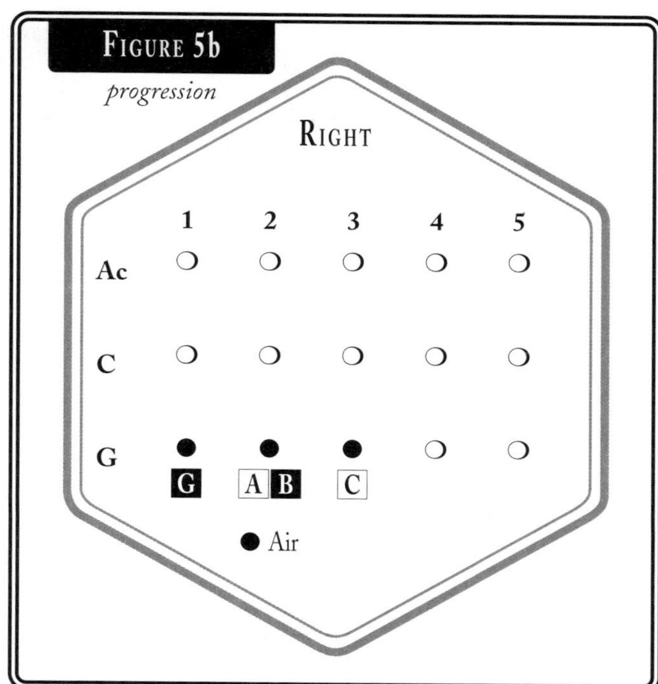

Key to symbols:

■ = pushed note; □ = pulled note;
1, 2, etc = button number; ● = button pushed or pulled;
1, 2, etc = finger
Ac = accidentals row; **C** = C row; **G** = G row

Out on the ocean

Track 4

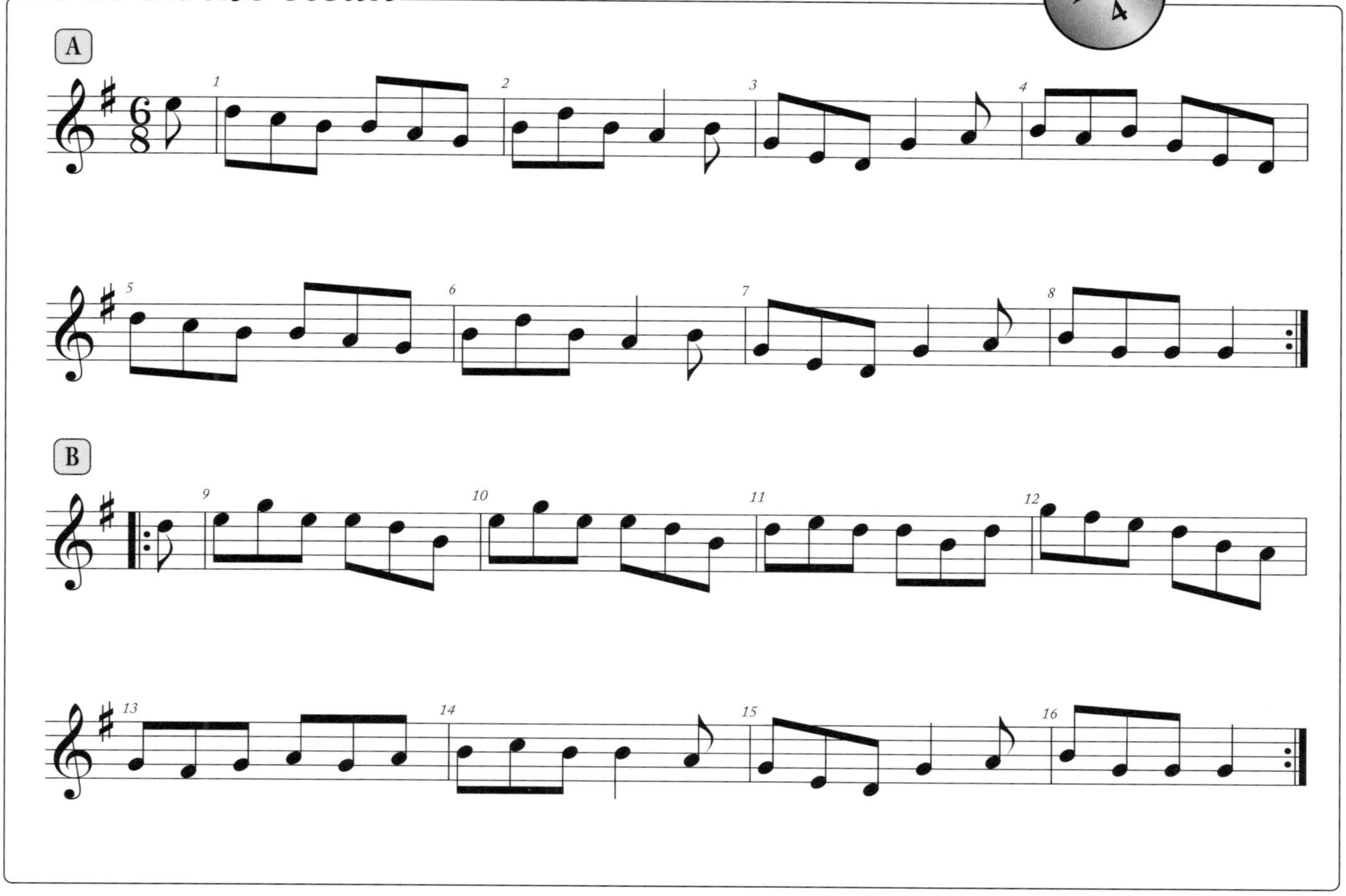

A

B

The kesh jig

Track 5

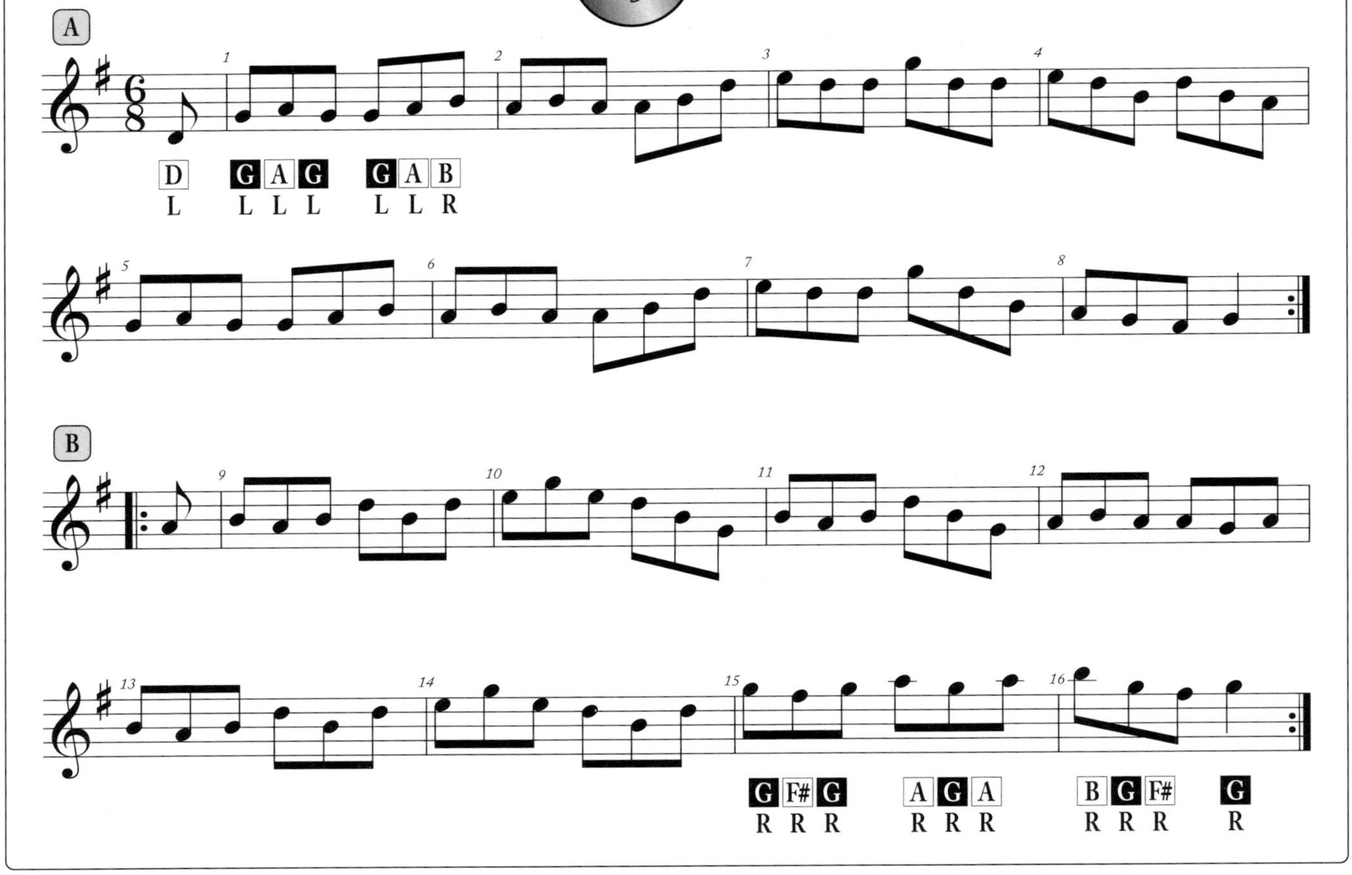

A

D L | G L A L G L | G L A L B R

B

G R F# R G R | A R G R A R | B R G R F# R | G R

The morning star

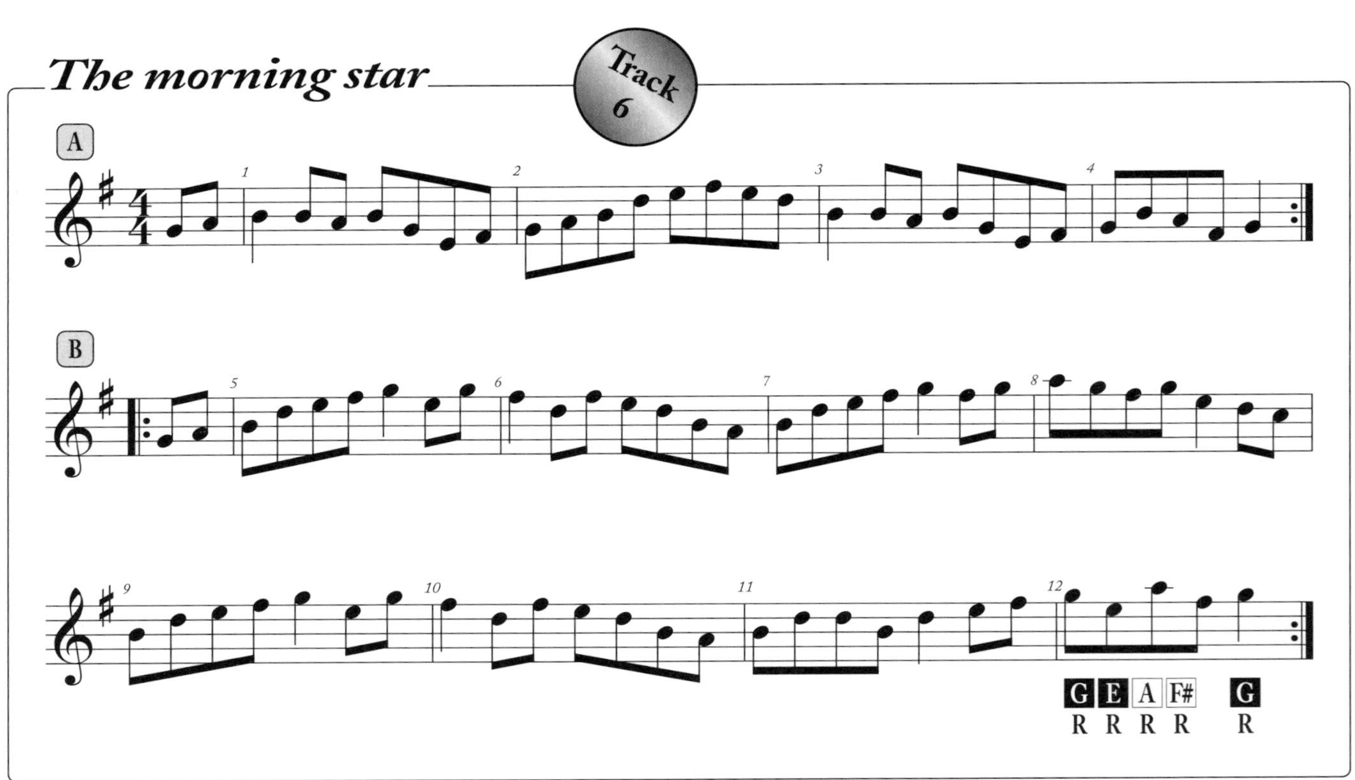

Some tips on air control

Something I have not touched on yet is air control. Each instrument is individual in its air requirements and you will know those needs from having practised with your particular model (see the section 'Choosing the right instrument', page 2). By using a push-pull technique at first, you will probably not need to use the air control for a turn through the tune. There will obviously be exceptions to this rule if there are leaks in the instrument but if your box is air efficient then you will proceed with ease. Should you need air, then attempt to allow it out of the bellows while on the push. Allowing it in when pulling usually creates the problem of running out of air completely as the bellows reach full stretch. It can also be stressful to old bellows on the less expensive instruments.

When playing in the key of G major, it is necessary to admit air into the bellows before playing the scale. Open the bellows about halfway and the push-pull system for this first exercise will not require any more air control. With the second method for G major, you will not need to use the air button for a couple of runs through the scale both up and down but in a short while you will find that the bellows are becoming extended; if you do not do something about air availability, then you will reach full stretch. It is quite easy to revert to a push on the first button, left-hand C row and include a half-open air button to expel enough air to continue the scale in both directions. Air can be expelled at any note on the push.

With D major, the same rule applies. There is no need to stretch the bellows as the first note in the left hand is pulled. To expel excess air, try using a half-open air button when pushing the second note of the scale, E on the C row, when or if the bellows begin to get stretched.

Low notes which use large reeds on the C and accidental rows create the biggest headaches for air control. Try to pre-plan the admission of plenty of air before you get down to the bottom end of scales which use these notes. If a low note is to be pushed, then let air in with the previous pulled note. Do just the reverse if the low note is to be pulled.

For quiet passages, such as in slow airs or in a room where you are perhaps playing alone, it is possible to control volume by the use of the air button. As an exercise, play a pushed G on the C row, first button and depress the air button fractionally at the same time. The volume of the note should decrease as the air is expelled and increase as the air button is released.

Chords can be used effectively to either admit or expel air prior to a long run of notes. A good dodge for letting in plenty of air, especially at the end of a phrase, is to play a chord on the left-hand side; in the present exercise a chord of G major, as shown in *figures 6a* and *6b*.

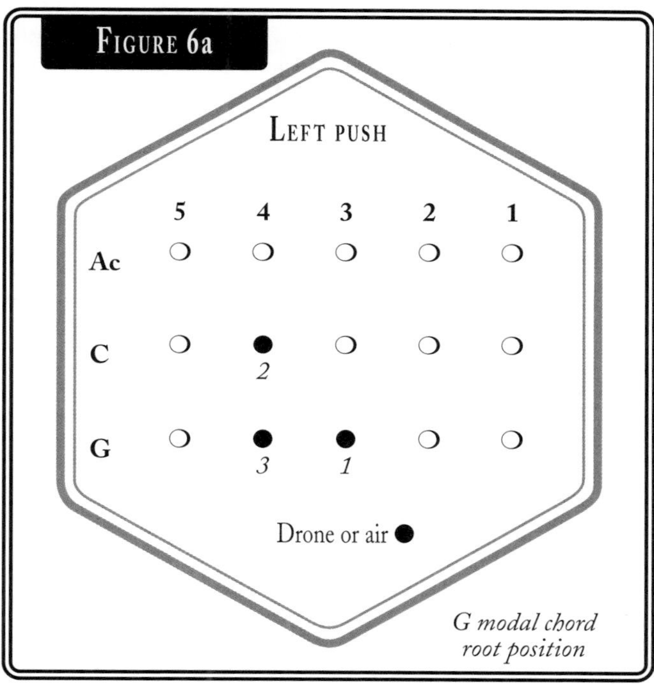

G modal chord root position

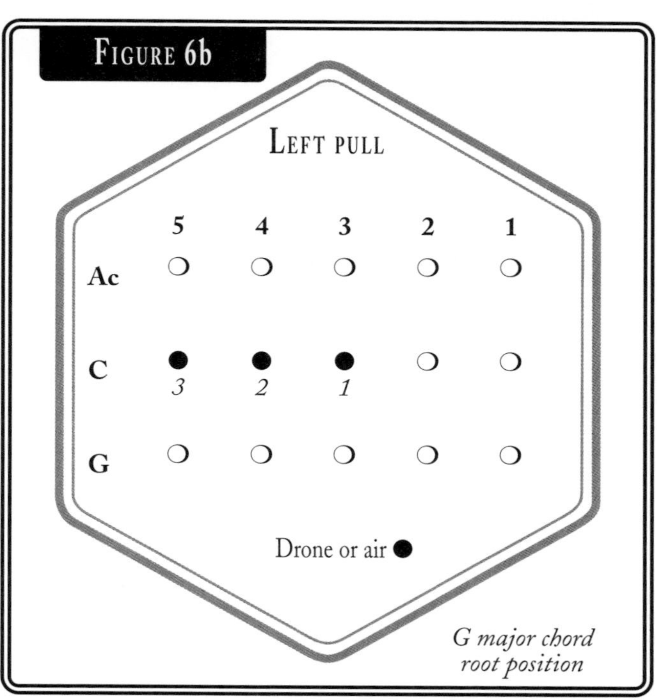

G major chord root position

A fuller chart of easily found chords is included in appendix three.

When you are confident that you can produce the scale for G major by pulling and pushing, there are two possible routes to choose from next:

1. *Go on to the key of D major using the same method,*
   or
2. *Learn another way of playing G major which will naturally increase the speed and fluidity of your style.*

If you want option 1, then turn to page 16.

Another way of playing G major

The scale of G major can be 'pulled' from the concertina without ***any*** change in direction of the bellows. It does require more control over the air button but it produces faster progression through the scale.

By referring to your layout chart, you will see that on the outside row of the instrument where the accidental notes occur, there are some notes duplicated from the two diatonic rows. The ones which concern us particularly at the moment are any spare (duplicated) Gs and As. As I have mentioned before, the layout of each instrument can vary slightly, so you must adapt the following information to your own needs even though the basic method remains the same.

Start by pulling the 2nd button down on the accidental row on the left-hand side. It should sound a G and you can check it by reverting to the left hand C row and pushing the 1st button. The sequence may best be described by *figure 7* as all the air is being pulled into the bellows.

The letters under the buttons show the order of playing. It will take a while for the above method to sink in; ***do*** play it slowly at first. As your confidence with the system builds then so will your speed of execution but keep an even beat at all times. If you start to lose control of your air, try playing the last note of the scale, G, by pushing the G button on the right-hand side C row as note 8. This fluid way of playing is certainly easier in G major than in other keys but it will be seen later that various scales can benefit from the technique.

In order to play the scale repeatedly, you can use a mixture of fluid pulling and a couple of pushes, as shown in *figure 8*. This will eradicate the air button in all probability. Push the left-hand G before commencing the scale by pulling the rest of the notes up to F♯, then push the final G.

Practise these styles until you find which one suits you and your concertina the best. Herein lies a warning! Do not take the easy option as the whole purpose of this book and the method it contains is supposed to break you of such behaviour. By reversing the scale and starting at the top, you should be able to join the two directions as a single, flowing line of music which gains in speed as you gain in confidence. It should sound rather like a peal of bells.

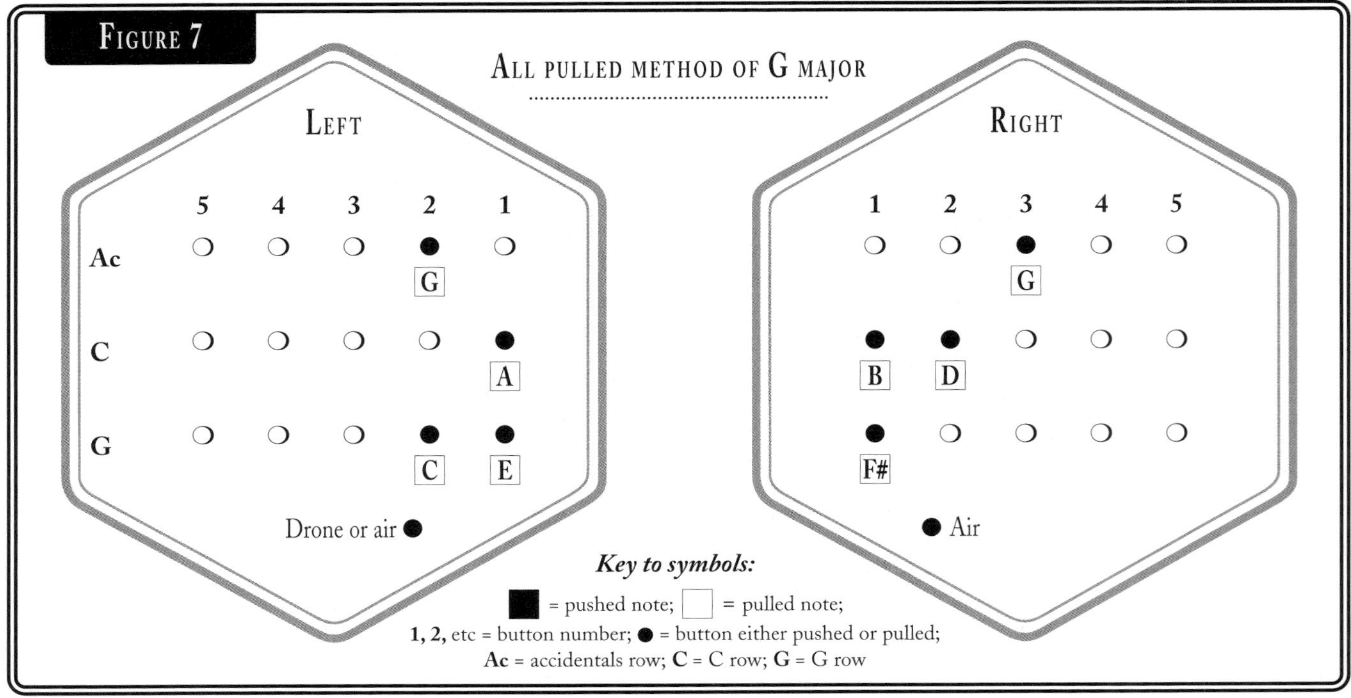

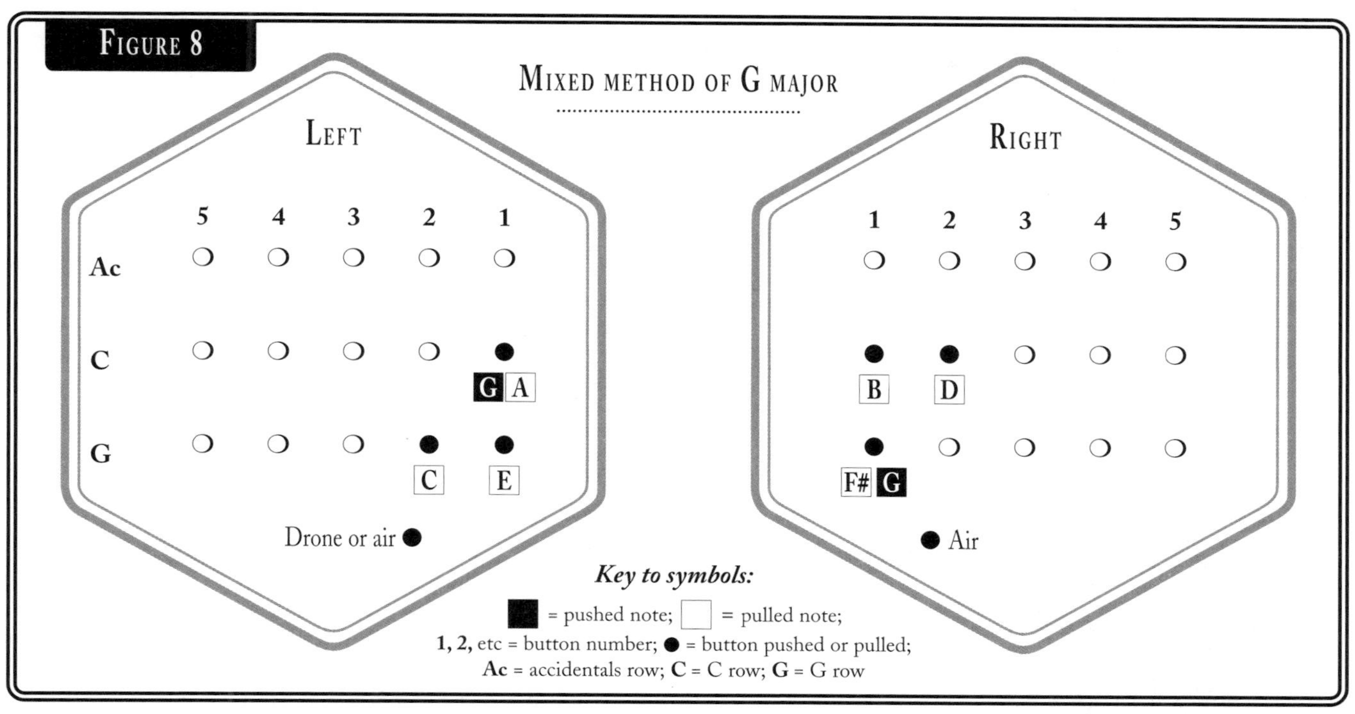

Linda Bramich

A famous venue for Irish music in Westport, County Mayo

THE KEY OF D MAJOR

D major is a favourite key for many musicians. In order to achieve it on a G/C instrument you must be prepared to work very much harder than for the scale of G major.

Two accidental notes must be brought into play: F♯ and C♯. They both occur on the three-row Anglo, the F♯ as you already know on the G row and the C♯, as you may have guessed, on the accidental row. The most useful C♯s fall on the right-hand side, on the two buttons shown in *figure 9.* One of them is a push note and the other is a pull. You must find out which way your box is configured before embarking on the next stage. I will illustrate the method as it falls under the fingers on my own concertina but I will also endeavour to include technique for the other common layout.

I will start with a straightforward exercise—*figure 10*—that will climb the accepted scale of D major with two sharps in one or both direction(s). Take up the left-hand finger positions as for G major. Pull the 3rd button down, on the C row, to sound D, using the third finger. Push the next button up to sound E; pull the F♯ on the G row; push the G on the C row. You are half way there! Pull the A on the left hand C row; pull B on the right hand C row; now pull the C♯ on the accidental row (this could be either of the first two buttons) and pull the D on the C row to finish.

Practise this scale carefully and slowly. As your manual dexterity improves, try coming down the scale. You will notice that C♯ is available as a pushed note on one of the first two accidental buttons of the right-hand side. This can be used rather as in the G scale as a method of conserving or releasing air.

Extending beyond the top and bottom of a one octave scale in D major brings some pitfalls. The fluidity of the scale becomes interrupted by the many changes in bellows direction needed to complete the exercise.

The next example, *figure 11,* takes you a further octave up the scale. You start by sounding the D on the right-hand C row and following the diagram from there. For the lower end of the scale, you will probably find that your instrument cannot complete an octave below the D on the C row in the left hand. *Figure 12* on page 18 gives the layout common to many Anglos that I have played upon.

As you will note, a low G is as far as one can get, the next available note being an F natural on the accidental row, followed by an E. I would be surprised if you ever needed to go below the A on the accidental row when playing in this key. The fingers you choose to sound these notes are left largely up to you and what you find most comfortable; it is worth noting that fiddle players move their left hand into higher positions to reach the extended range of their instruments. By moving your right hand up the end of the concertina, as in *figures 13a* and *13b,* you can achieve similar results given the extra flexibility now open to you.

On page 19 are two tunes which exploit the method in the key of D major. They are not furious reels but a gentle hornpipe (a very nice form for concertina playing) and a double jig.

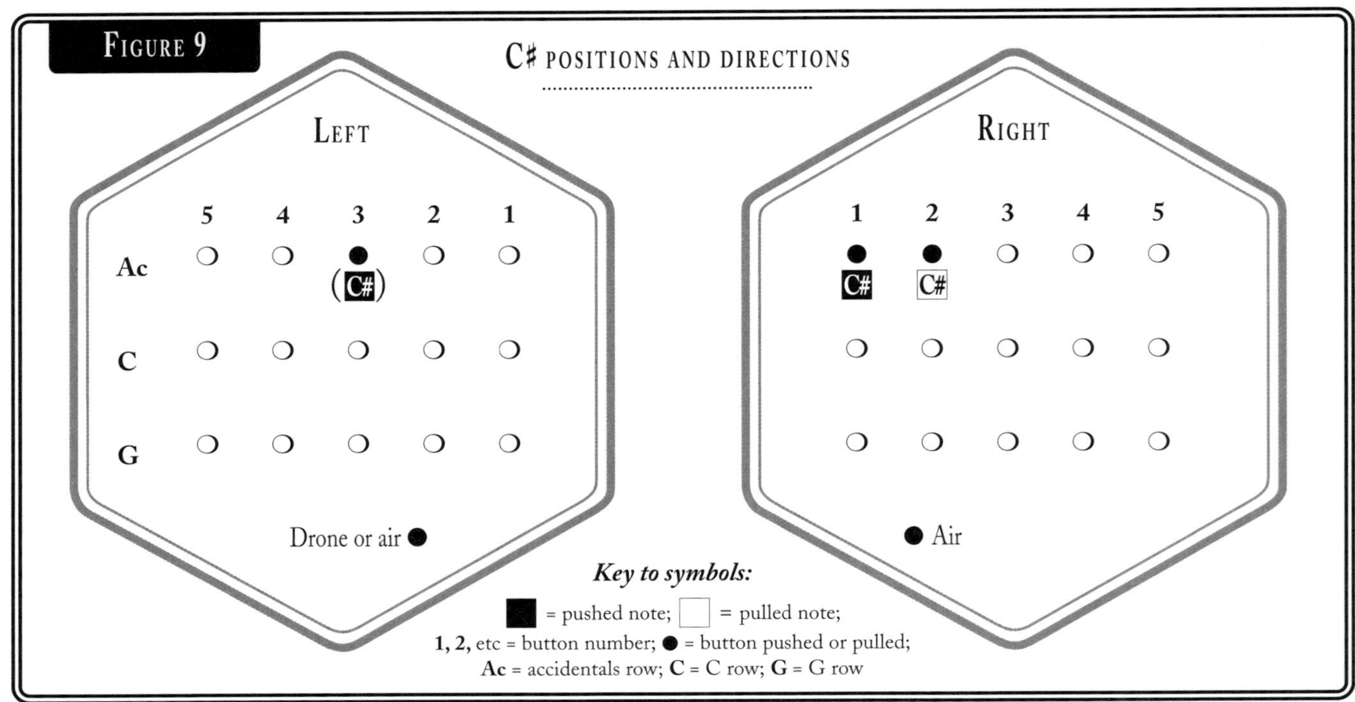

The scale of D and button positions

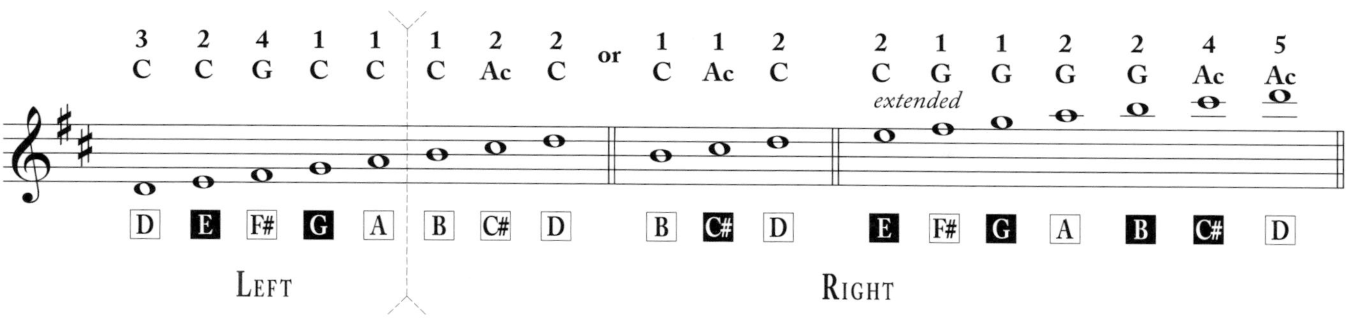

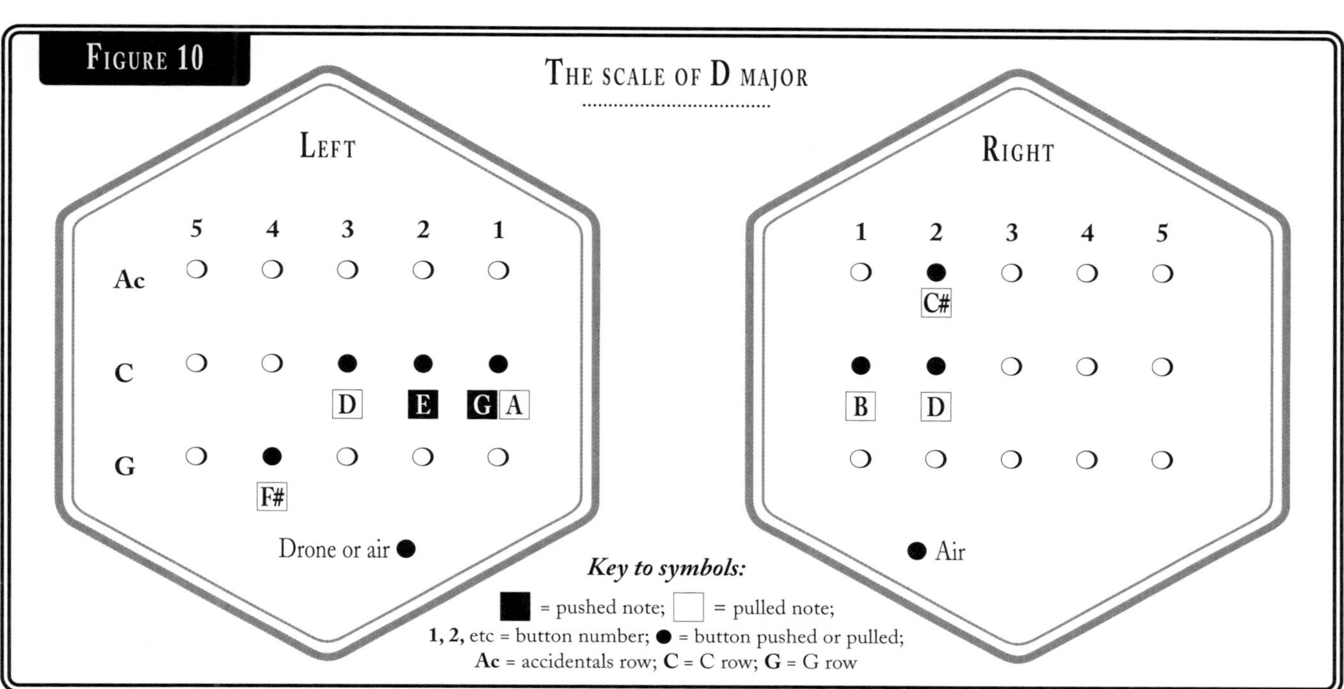

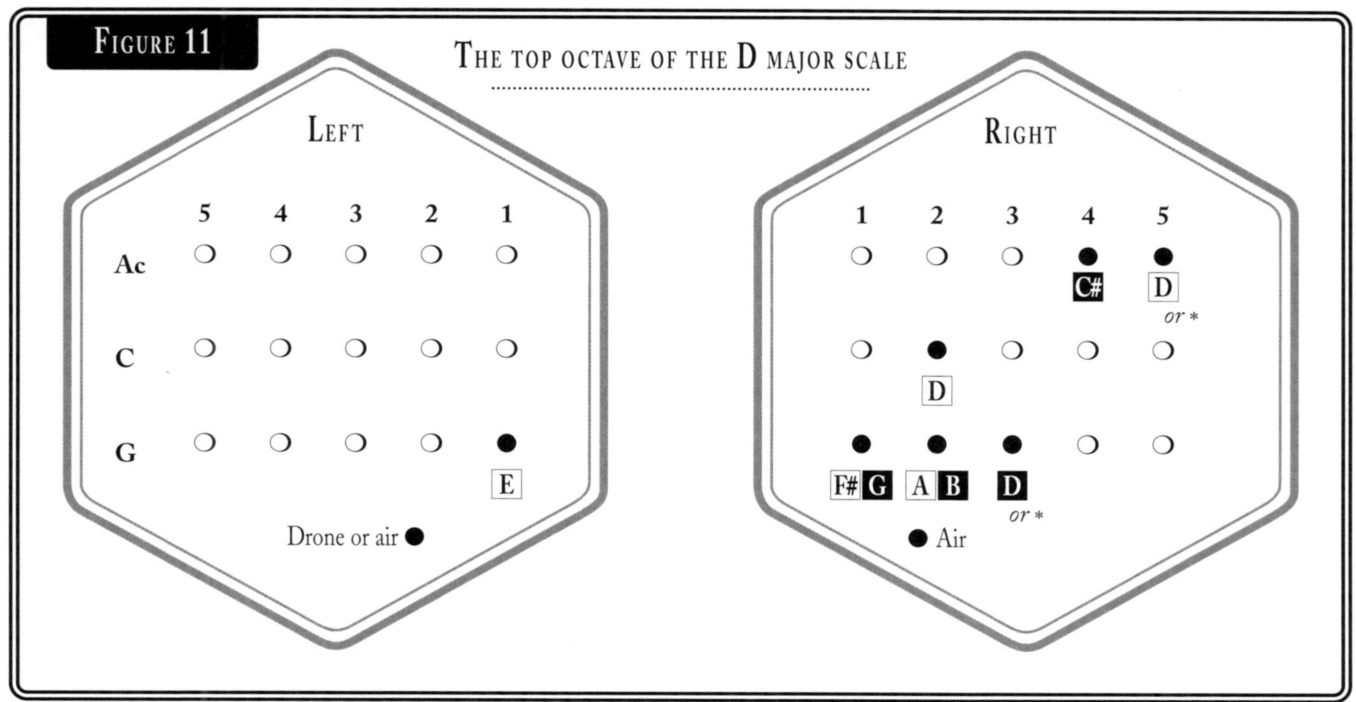

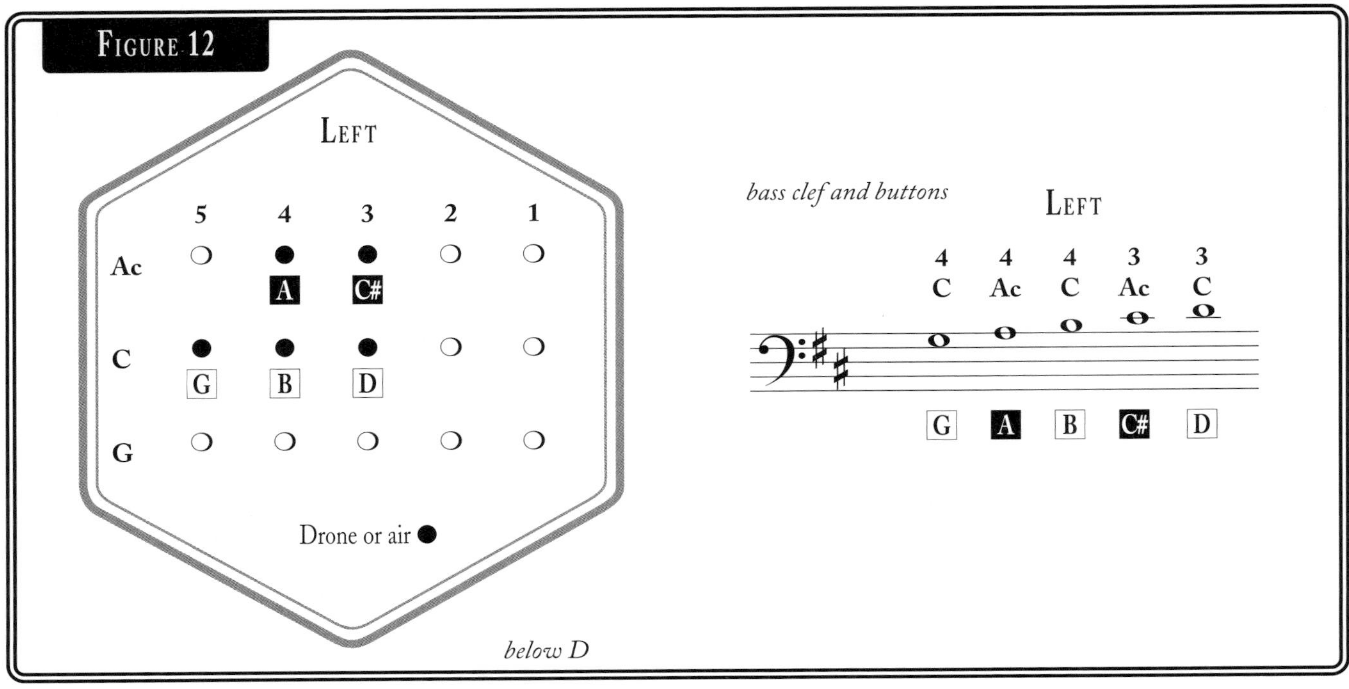

Key to symbols:

■ = pushed note; □ = pulled note;

1, 2, etc = button number; ● = button pushed or pulled;

1, 2 etc = finger

Ac = accidentals row; **C** = C row; **G** = G row

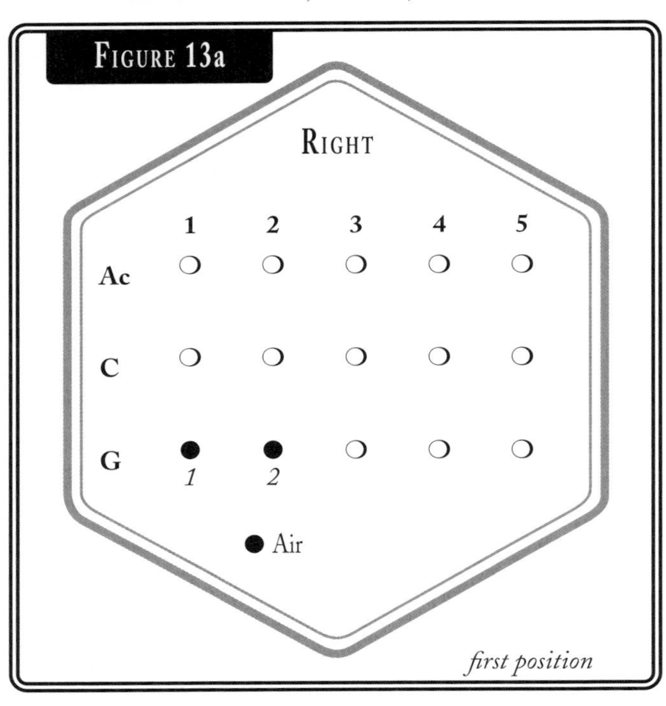

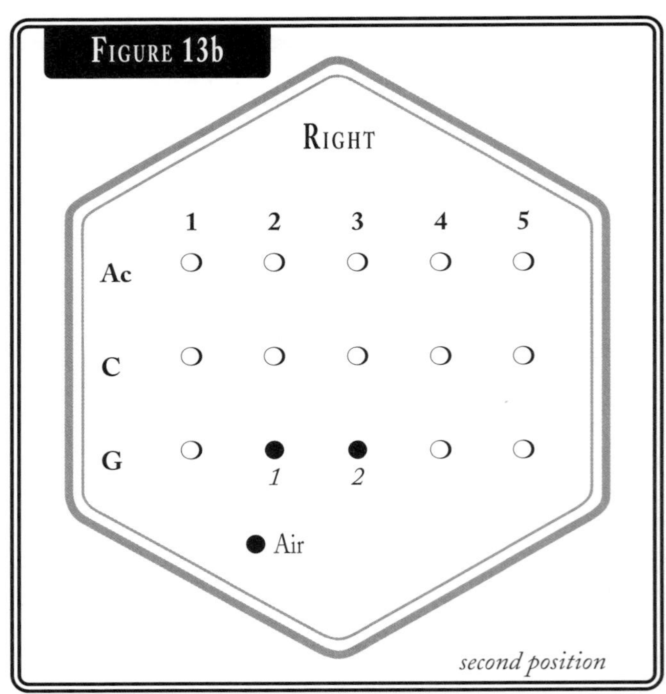

The boys of Bluehill

Track 7

A

B

The Kinnegad slashers

Track 8

A

B

Scales

Let us back-pedal a little and look at melodic and harmonic scales. We will look at the scale of A minor as it will lead neatly into the next set of exercises.

You will see from the diagrams below that the harmonic form is the same in both directions whereas the melodic scale is different depending upon direction. Even though it is accepted that there are no sharps or flats in this key, the seventh in the harmonic and (when climbing the scale) the sixth and seventh in the melodic are sharpened and should be written as such on the stave.

C major however has no sharps or flats and although related to A minor does not display sharpened sixths or sevenths. In traditional music, neither of the scales shown in *figures 14a* and *b* are found with any regularity as they pertain mainly to 'art' music. Much of our native music contains only the sharpened sixth, in this case, F♯. There are a few tunes that show the melodic structure when descending but even these are rare. This quirk is in part to do with the 'modal' nature of traditional music. The key of A minor as found in the majority of printed and oral sources occurs in the dorian mode; the intervals between the notes can be clearly defined from the *figure 14c.*

Try not to get bogged down on theory at the moment but I will ask you to play these scales after we have examined the method for A minor in more detail. So, now onto that most melancholy of scales, A minor, with its capacity to make grown men weep when applied to the concertina.

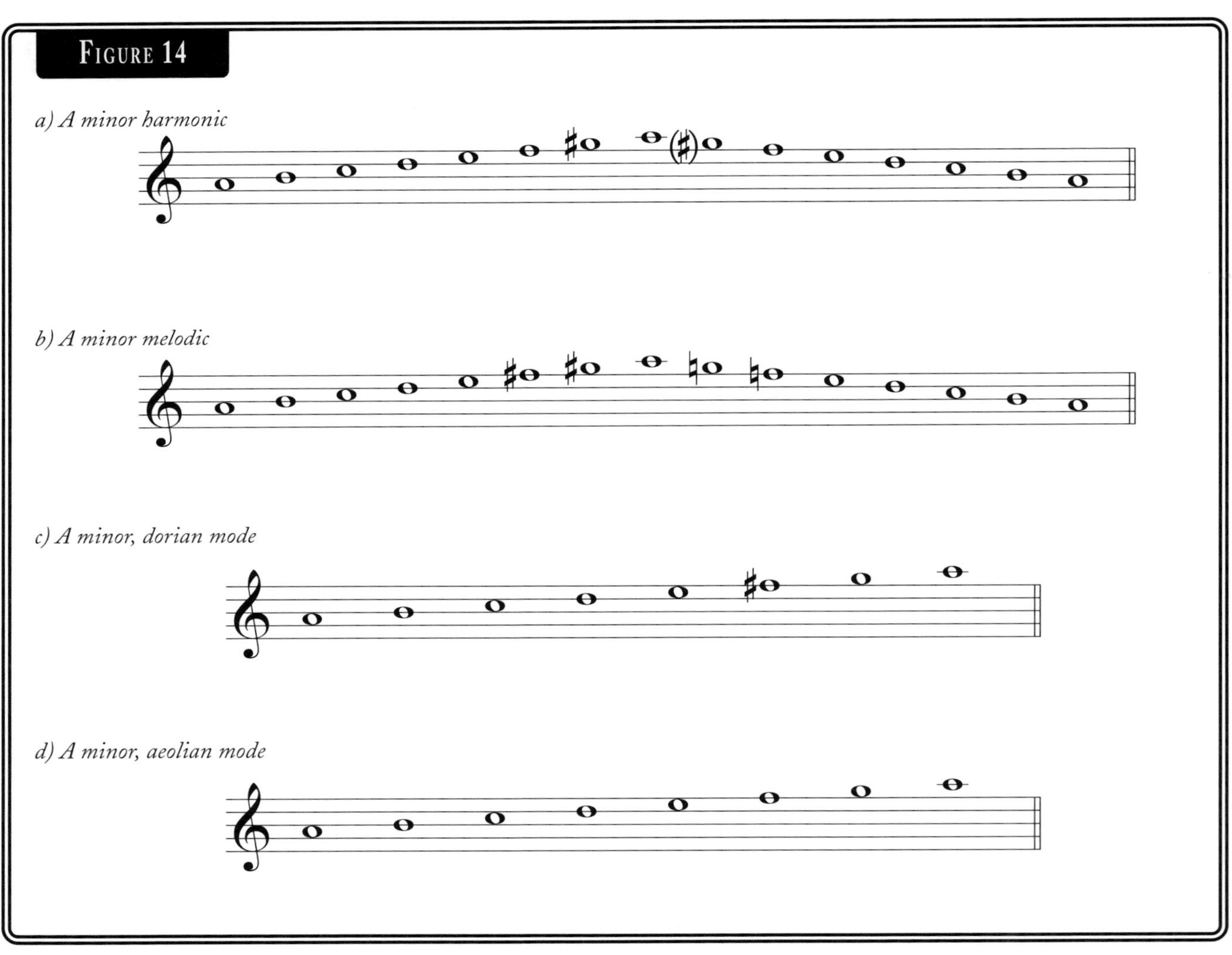

THE KEY OF A MINOR

Many traditional tunes occur in the key of A minor. They seem to impart a longing for something lost and distant, perhaps the common man's yearning for his homeland or a sorely missed loved one. Whatever the formula is, the tunes are modal in nature.

As discussed earlier, the majority are to be found in the dorian mode, that is, with a sharpened sixth - F♯. Some, however, have no sharps or flats and are thus in the aeolian mode (*figure 14d,* previous page). As before, we will look at the fingering method and attempt to make the scale flow freely from the instrument.

Figure 15 below shows the push and pull method, which is entirely on the C row; so it should be, it being the relative minor to the key of C major. Start by pulling the A on the left-hand side; by now you should know that it is the topmost button on the C row. Continue to pull the B on the right-hand side; push for C; pull the next for D; push for E; pull the next for F natural; push for G and finish with a pull on the fourth button to sound A one octave above the start of the scale. It is here that we must introduce an F♯ into the proceedings in order to cover the variations which occur within the body of collected traditional music. So, follow the directions up to the push for E, then drop onto the G row first button to pull an F♯. Finish Off by pressing the same button for G and pulling an A from the second button on the G row. See *figure 16* overleaf. It is within A minor tunes that melodic forms start to appear in printed collections of music and in *Appendix one* you will find a couple of examples. But not now; try the pieces overleaf for practise.

Again, they are jigs, as they are good melodies for practise on the concertina. They flow a little easier than reels but with time, you will get into $\frac{4}{4}$. ***The rakes of Kildare*** has only the notes E and G in the left hand which fall outside the octave scale. There is one above the octave, that of B in the right hand. You should be able to find these by now without much trouble. ***The tenpenny bit*** is yet another well known session jig. As with the previous tune, the scale is extended but not difficult; note that it uses the G and the A on the accidental row in the left hand.

Figure 17 on page 23 shows that the scale of A minor dorian mode (and indeed the aeolian) can be pulled out of the instrument. Try to read the method straight from the diagram and practise the same two jigs to get used to the different system.

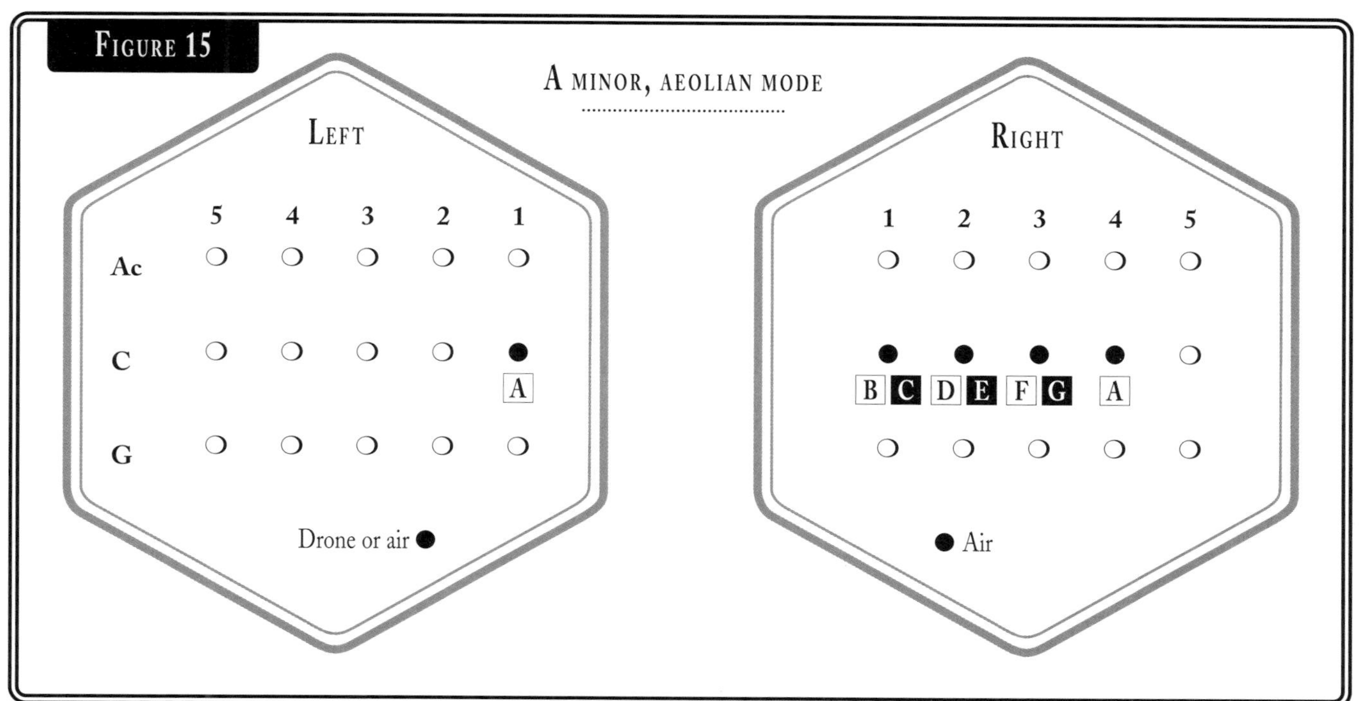

Key to symbols:

■ = pushed note; □ = pulled note;
1, 2, etc = button number; ● = button either pushed or pulled;
Ac = accidentals row; **C** = C row; **G** = G row

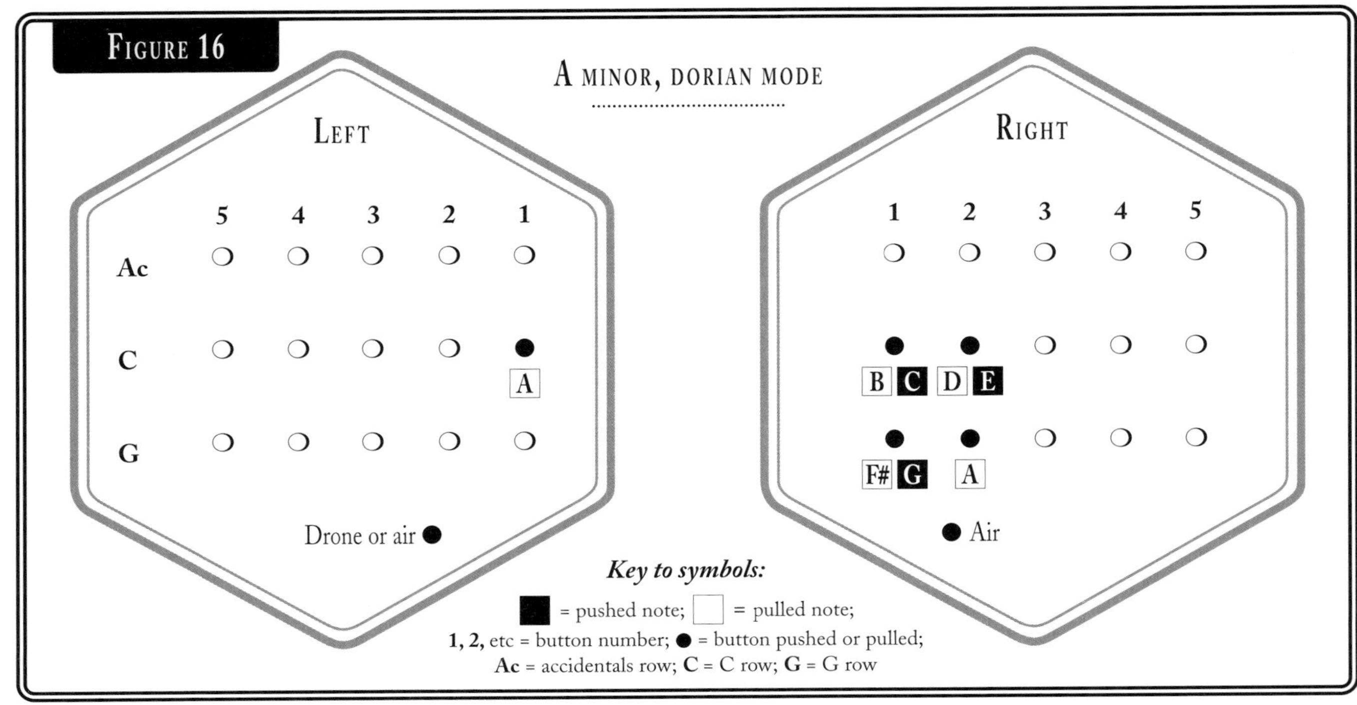

The rakes of Kildare

Track 9

A

A | E A A | A G A
L | L L L | L L L

B

A | A E A | A E A | B
R | R L R | R L R | R

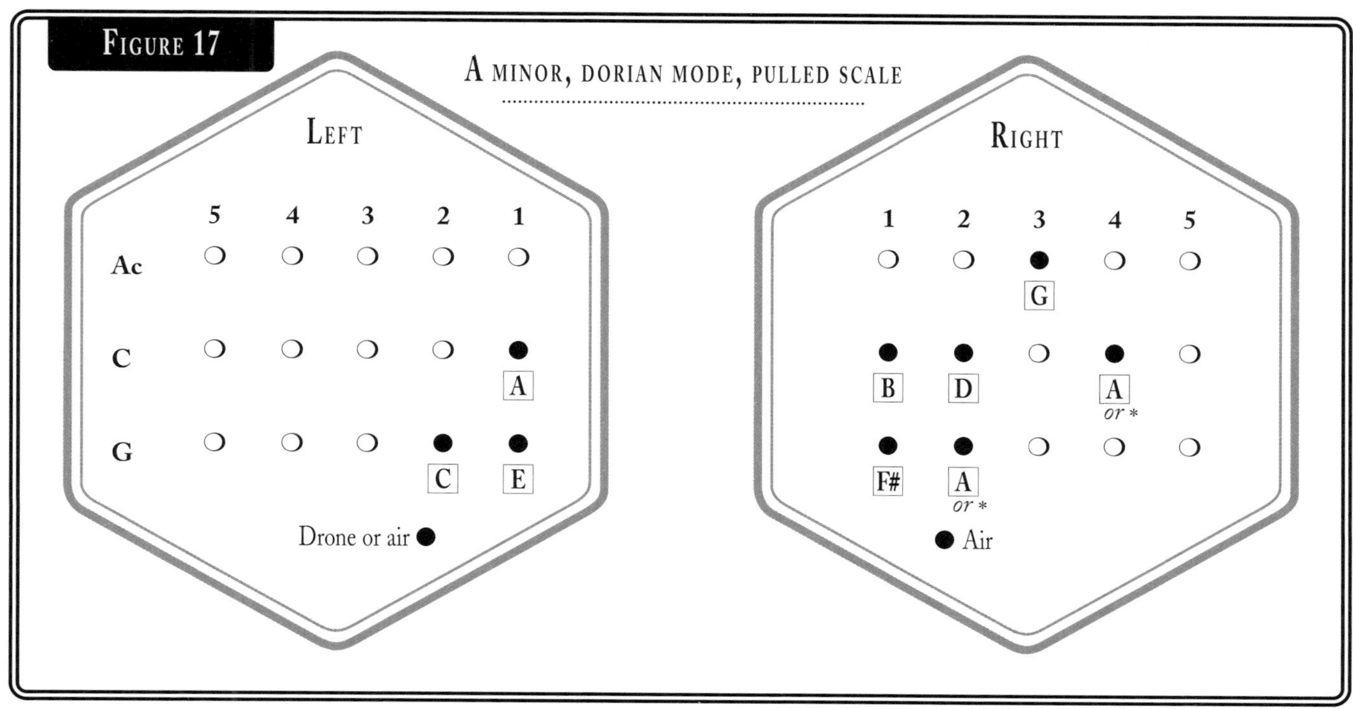

Key to symbols:

■ = pushed note; □ = pulled note;
1, 2, etc = button number; ● = button pushed or pulled;
Ac = accidentals row; **C** = C row; **G** = G row

The tenpenny bit

Track 10

A

E A A E A A B A B G B D D E F#
L L L L R L R L R R R L R
or A A A A G

B

THE KEY OF E MINOR

Just as A minor is related to C major, so E minor is related to G major. This does not mean, however, that we can play most of it on the G row. This is because of the influence of C♯ within the scale.

The key is approached in a similar way to that of D major; lots of changes in direction and the numbers of rows utilised.

You should now be able to follow diagrams quite well and I do not intend to make this and the following sections so wordy. The two versions of the scale shown in *figures 18* and *19* should be learned and practised. Do not forget what has gone before! Constant revision and exercise is essential prior to moving along the route to ever more complex situations.

The rights of man (see page 26) has an extended scale - as shown in *figure 20* - in the right hand and it also shows characteristics of both aeolian and dorian modes. The fingering for the higher notes is shown below the appropriate bars. Few E minor tunes drop below the D on the 3rd button of the left-hand C row although some decoration encompasses use of the accidental row.

Richard Branich

A session at the Bay Horse, Totnes, Devon

A group of close musician friends in Devon. For providing such valuable accompaniments, thanks go to Andy Clarke (banjo), Frank Moulder (mandolin), Bob Stevens (guitar), Ronnie Best (bodhrán), Tim West (fiddle) and Tim Wallace-Murphy (vocals & stories)

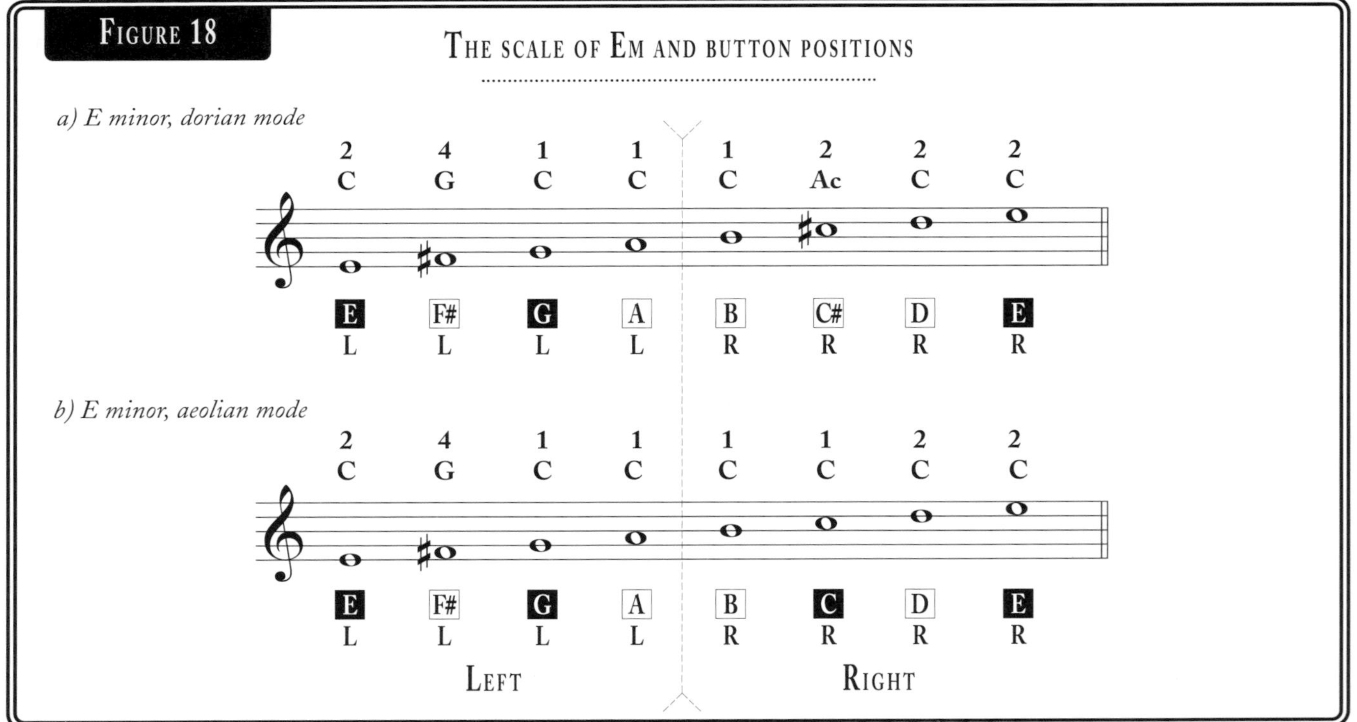

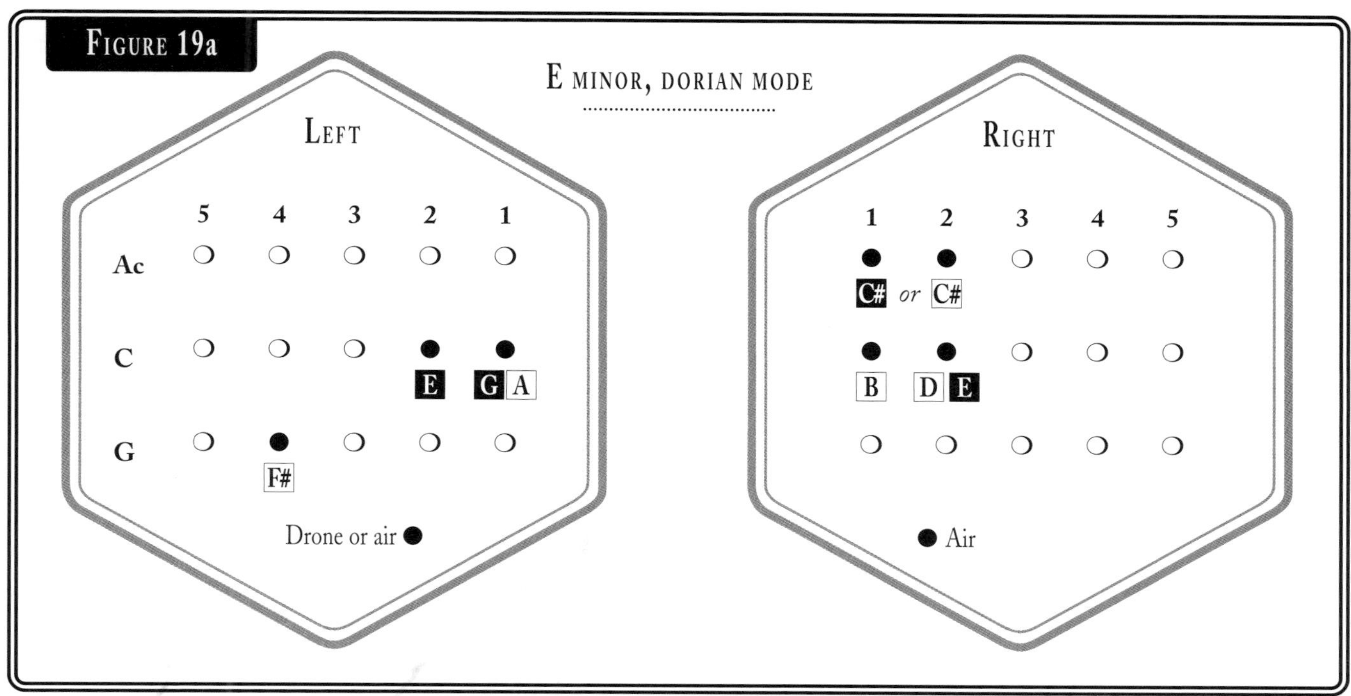

Key to symbols:

■ = pushed note; □ = pulled note;
1, 2, etc = button number; ● = button pushed or pulled;
Ac = accidentals row; **C** = C row; **G** = G row

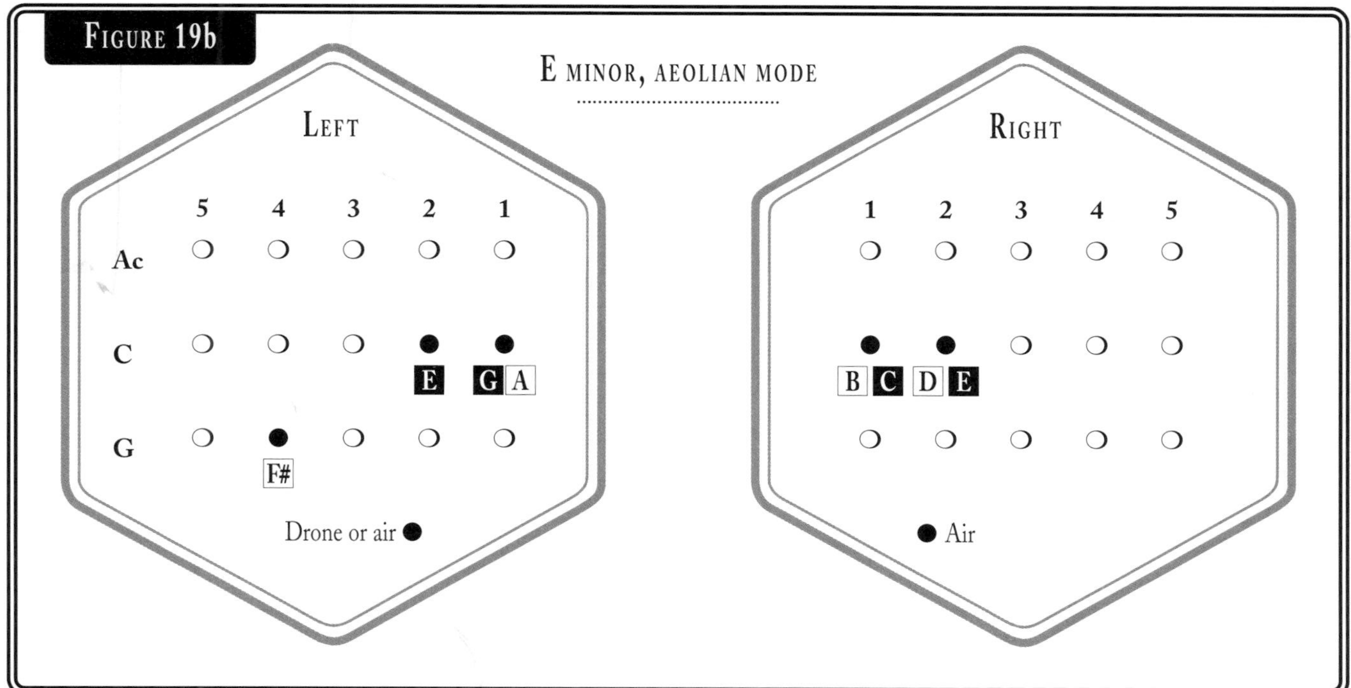

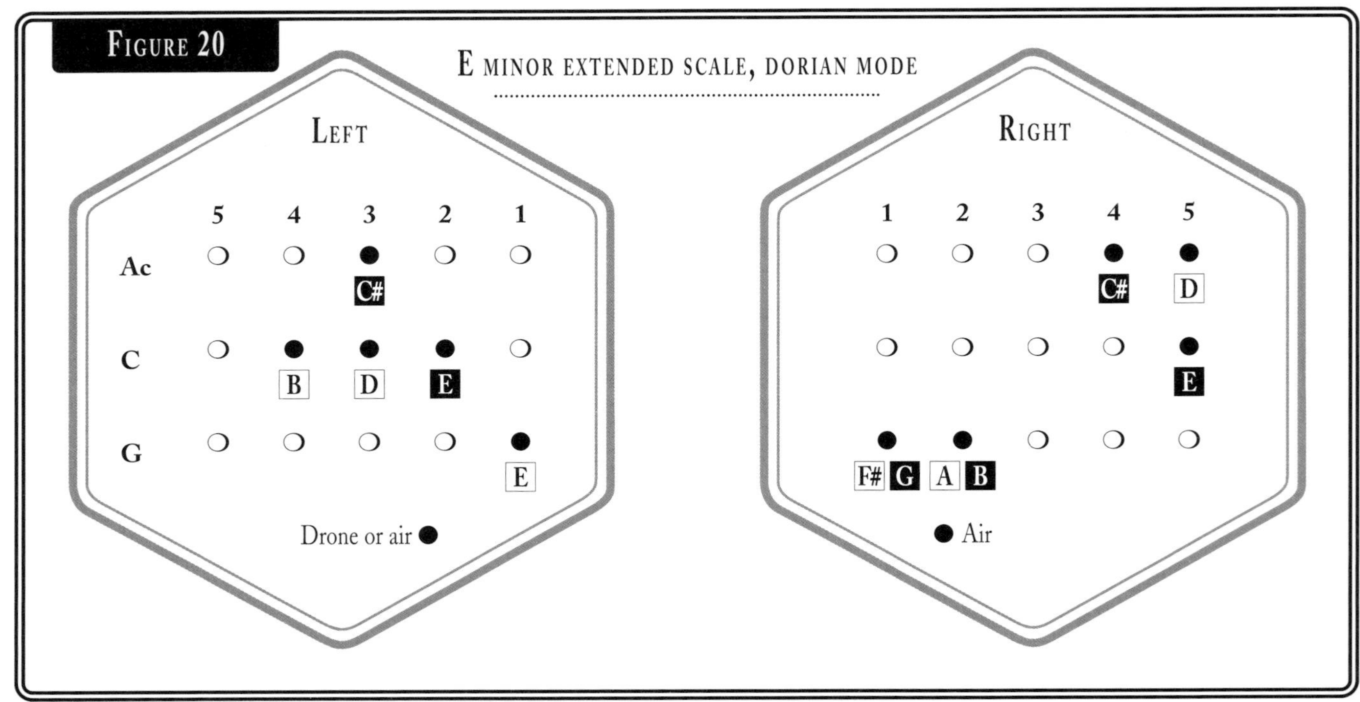

Figure 20

E minor extended scale, Dorian mode

Key to symbols:

■ = pushed note; □ = pulled note;
1, 2, etc = button number; ● = button pushed or pulled;
Ac = accidentals row; **C** = C row; **G** = G row

The rights of man

Track 11

A

B

D D C#
R R R

A F# B F#
R R R R

B G A F#
R R R R

The top of Maol

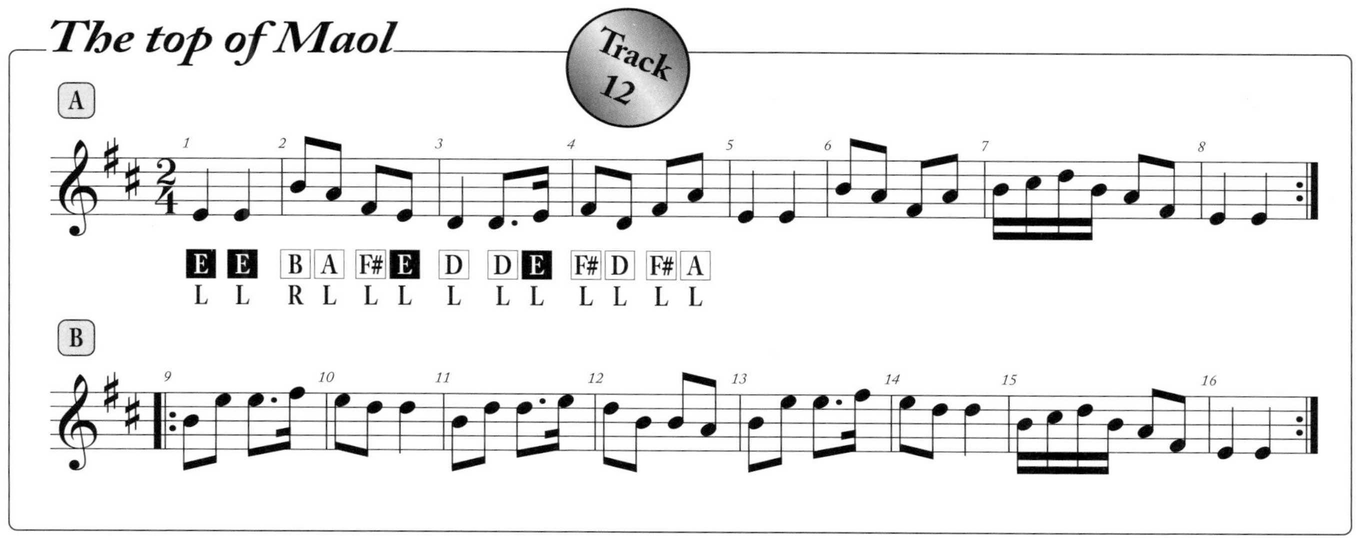

Apples in winter

Track 13

A

B

B G B A F# A
R R R R R R

Modulation

Thus far, we have concentrated on the method for playing tunes in one key, A minor for example. Much of our native traditional music gains its character from modulation; that is, changing from one key to another during the course of the melody line. It has nothing to do with harmony at this point. That is yet another mine-field of theory which we do not need to tackle when discussing a melody line instrument.

Common modulations in traditional music are from D minor to D major (and back again in all probability); G major to D major; A minor to C major; D major to B minor etc. You will recognise then, that there will be problems in changing from one key to another as it will inevitably involve changing method as well. Do not be put off by the inclusion of B minor in the above list as it is relative to D major and is covered in depth in a later section of this tutor.

At the risk of becoming repetitive, I will not give you diagrams to describe the changes but am happy to leave it up to you to make the necessary adjustments in playing the following examples of tunes which modulate. Once more, take things one step at a time, slowly and with caution in mind. Forget about trying to outgun Noel Hill (see *Appendix seven*) and simply learn the system at your own pace. Nobody is out there to get you or get at you as a novice in this style.

Both melodies, shown opposite, are clearly marked to show you the points of modulation and the keys involved.

The first or 'A' part of ***The hag with the money*** belongs to the pull and push method for the key of D minor. Note that there are no B♭ notes in this tune although technically speaking the key signature should show one flat. Simplification of the engraving of music often takes place in traditional music. In the 'B' music you can pull all the notes as far as bar number 14 and the air modulates again in bar 15 and you go back to pull and push. The asterisks show where the C♯s and F♯s arrive to make the tune major. The C natural in bar 15 takes it in and out of the minor very cleverly. ***Drowsy Maggie*** looks as if the whole tune is in D major but upon closer inspection you will see that the melody line begins on E, a reasonable indication that it is in E minor. It modulates to D major in bar 5, the tell-tale sign being the jump to a note of D.

A Jeffries F/B♭ from 1905

And now, here are a few basic exercises to consider:

1. Using the method for G major, fit some tunes that you already know into the extended scale (low D to A above G on the right-hand G row);
2. Transfer some A minor tunes into this method from the up and down the row, push-pull system;
3. Pay more attention to the use of the air control and keep referring back to the section on the use of air;
4. Repeat the above operations in the keys of D major and E minor and
5. Practise modulations in the established scales and find more examples for yourself.

Beyond the basic keys for traditional music

There are many pieces of music from the tradition that do not fit into the moulds of G, D, A minor and E minor. I hinted at this in the previous paragraphs on modulation. The Anglo concertina is, strictly speaking, a chromatic instrument; that is, it is possible to play in any key because of the range of accidental notes on the outside, third row.

The reality is very different however and you will come across some immense problems if trying to tackle such keys as E major, B major, F minor etc. So, forget them, as they seldom appear in traditional music and you can be sure that if they do, then they have more than likely been arranged by some learned theoretician with little interest in the true character of the music. The early folk song collectors were particularly guilty on this count and often re-wrote the melodies that they had originally fought so hard to preserve in order to make them 'correct' musically. By doing so, they missed the essential ingredients out: those of surprise and innovation which cannot be expected to exist in 'real' music.

The bag with the money

Track 14

D minor to D major

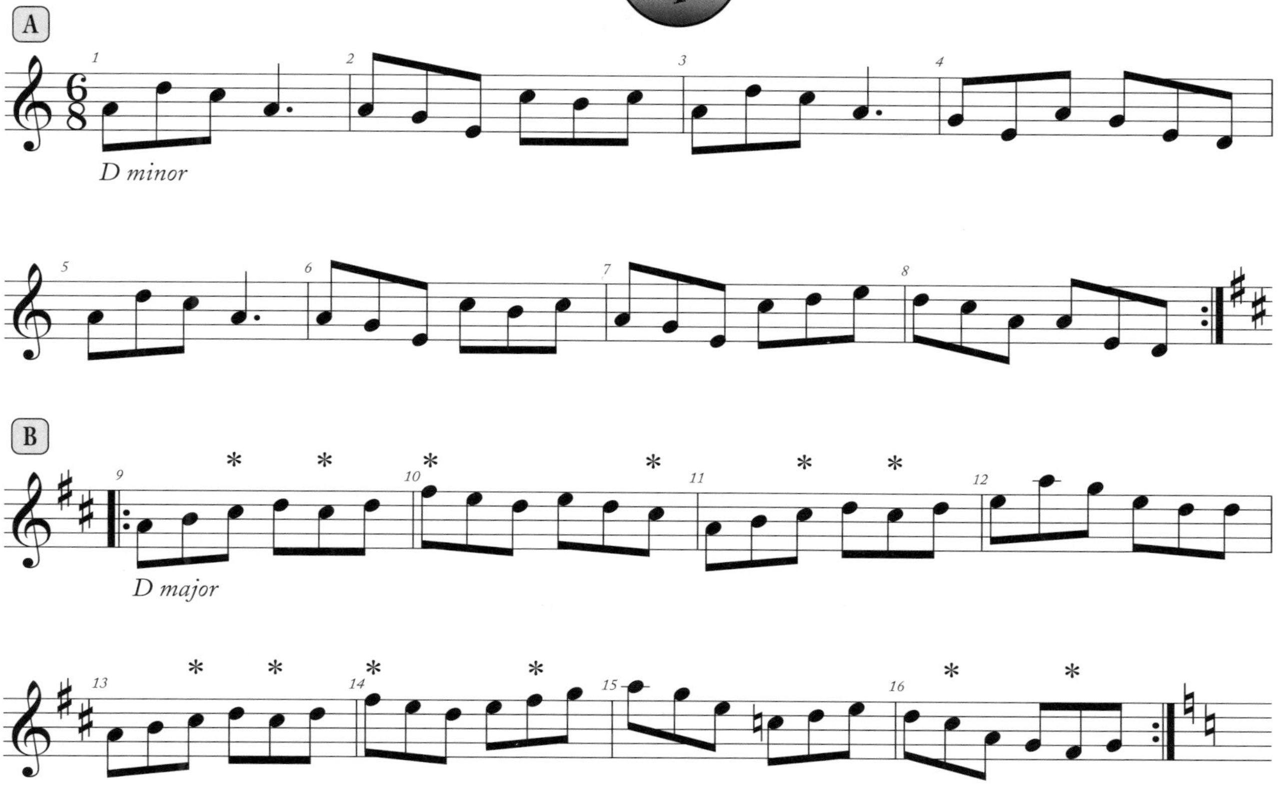

A

D minor

B

D major

The key of D minor

D minor contains one flat note, as does the key of F major which we will consider immediately after this section. B flat is available in several places on the left- and right-hand sides of the instrument. In the left hand, it occurs as the first accidental button on the pull. By playing this button in conjunction with the second one down on the C row, you will achieve a short form of the chord of B♭ major. This can be useful in the control of air into or out of the bellows while playing in this key.

The bulk of the notes are to be found on the C row but naturally start at a different point to the scale of C major. Rather like D major, the run starts by pulling the third button down on the C row to sound a D. Push the next for E; pull the same for F; push the next for G; pull for A (as an alternative you could move to the A on the accidental row and push). Now you must move to the B♭ on the accidental row and pull that note out of the box; push the C on the right-hand side and finally pull the D on the second button of the C row.

At this point, the difference between the aeolian and dorian modes can be looked at. Refer to *figures 21a* and *21b*. Some tunes written in the key of D minor do not contain any B flats.

As in previous exercises, practise the scale in both directions. Can you find any short cuts such as pulling the majority of the notes out to create the scale? Are there any real diffculties with air control?

The extension of this scale above and below the one octave - see *figure 22* - described here will depend upon the layout of your instrument. Some early models have a B♭ on the left-hand side as a pull on the fourth button down the accidental row. This can also be anything from B to E♭. Check your chart before attempting to go down on this side. On the right it is much more clearly defined and the flow of notes is relatively easy.

As with most scales on the left-hand side of the box, a full octave below the starting point, D in this case, cannot be achieved. You will note that a low E is as far as you can go but this is most unlikely to be required except perhaps in 'art' music settings or the creations of Tin Pan Alley. There is a C below that E on the accidental row but no D to fill the gap.

D minor tunes are not overabundant but do occur in older collections of Scottish and Irish music. The uilleann pipes which are termed 'flat' are generally tuned in the key of C major and therefore have a related minor of D. Shown opposite is ***Garrett Barry's jig***, a well known melody which can be found in D minor although, nowadays, it is usually played in the major with some modulation to C.

If you have any printed books of tunes, try scouring them for D minor melodies. Look for the B♭ on the stave but also recall that the tunes may not have any flats at all. One flat on the music stave can also refer to tunes in F major and so that will be the next key to consider.

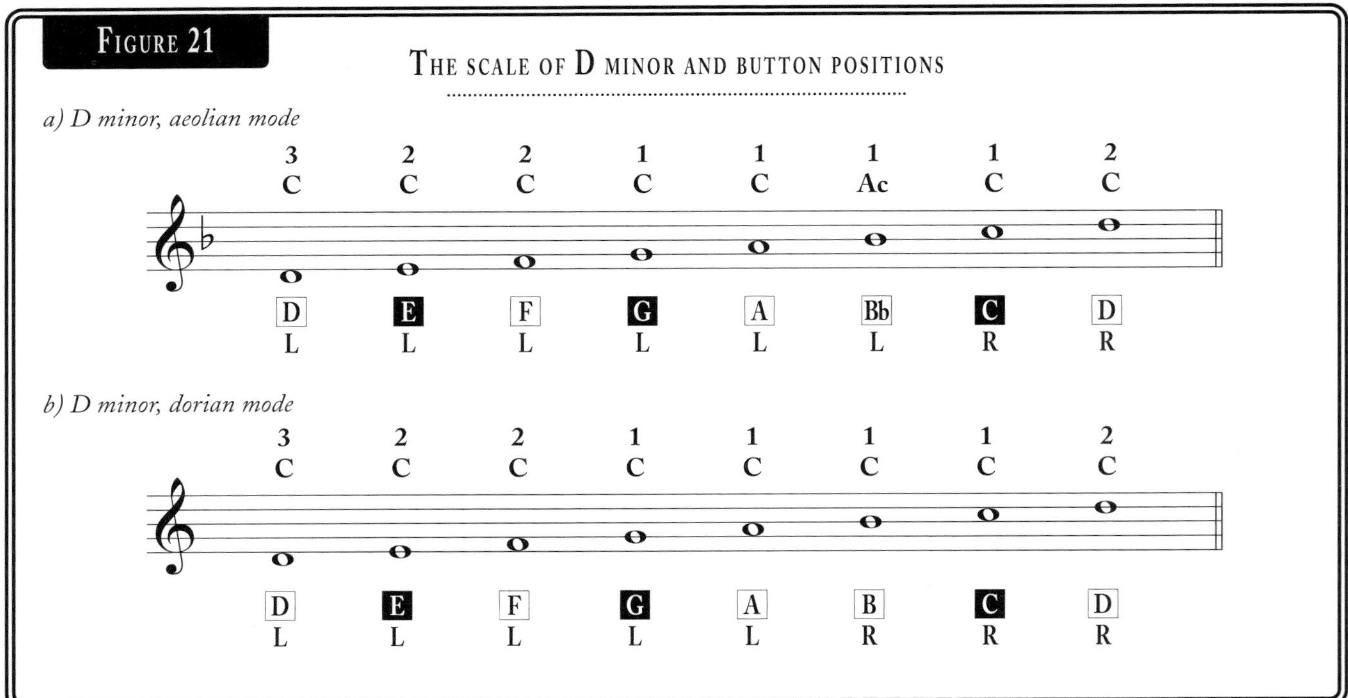

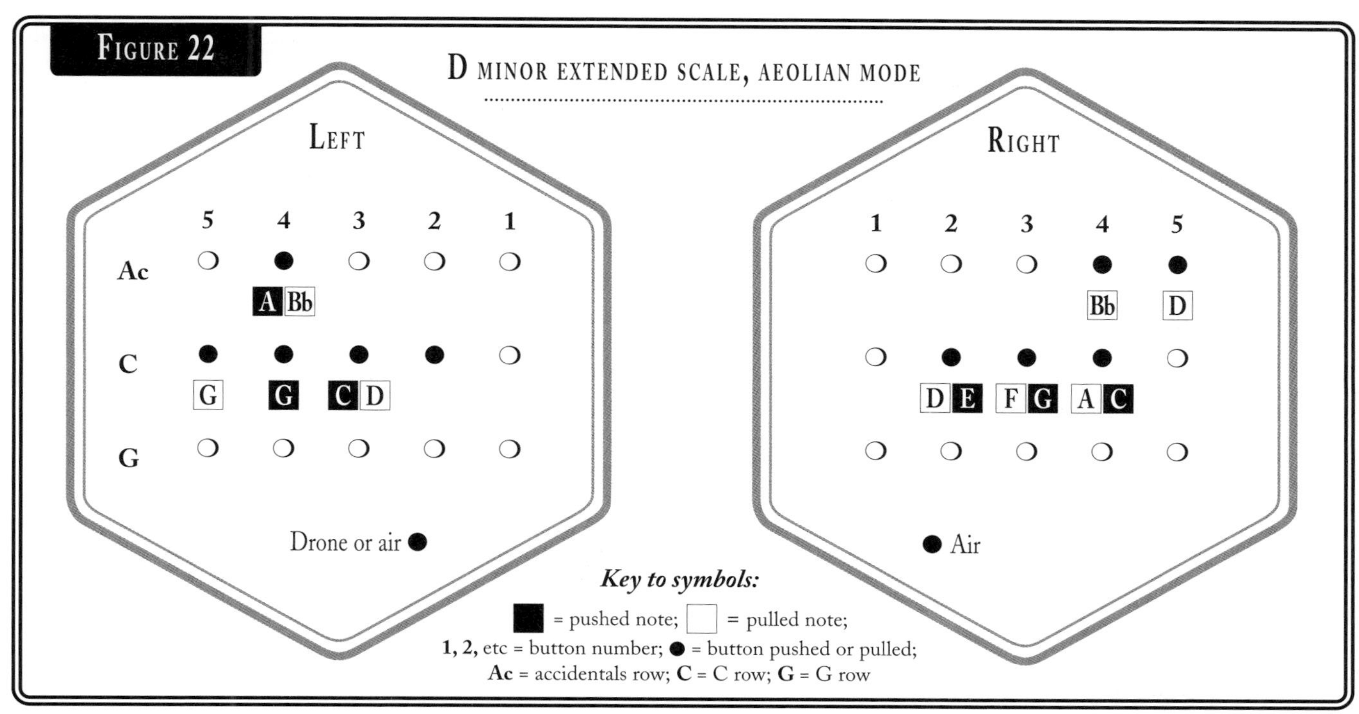

Garrett Barry's jig

Track 16

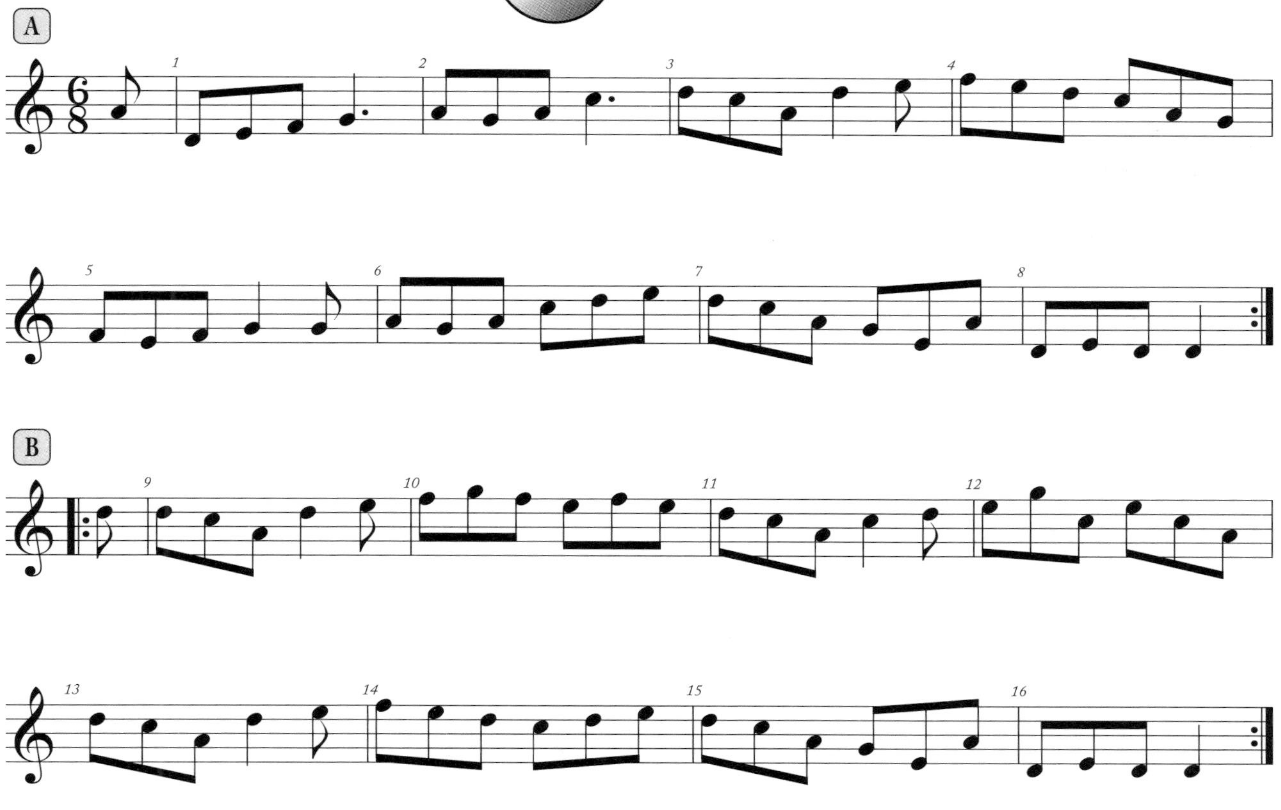

A

B

THE KEY OF F MAJOR

F major is found in collections of fiddle music. Pipers hate it; melodeon players (as opposed to button accordeon players) need a different box to play it on; flute and whistle players cringe at the thought of it. The competent Anglo player can be self-assured that he or she can simply change the fingering pattern and join in, even if solely to add a chord sequence to the melody.

F major contains one flat, that of B and because it is a major key, it can be assumed that the B♭ will be present in the bulk of tunes written in that key. Once again, the majority of the notes are to be found on the C row and it is only a short step from D minor to create the correct pattern of fingering.

Starting with the second button down on the left-hand C row, pull the note of F. There are two definite patterns which can take you to B♭. See *figure 23,* below right.

1 Pull F; push the by now familiar G button (the first on the C row); pull the same for A and then continue to pull the first accidental for B♭

or

2 Pull the F; push the G; change to the accidental row second button and push the A, then pull the B♭.

The fingering pattern for the second way is somewhat easier than it may appear on paper and the flow of the scale is much smoother than in 1.

On the right-hand side it is a very straightforward run up the scale from C with a push; pull for D; push for E and finish with a pull for the F one octave above the starting point.

F major above the octave is fairly plain sailing, all on the pull (dependent upon your particular layout) and involves a comfortable fingering pattern. Pull the F on the third button on the right-hand C row; pull the third accidental for G; pull the fourth C row for A, then finish on the fourth accidental for B♭. Practise the extended upper scale in both directions.

In the left hand there is a complete octave below the starting point if your instrument has a B♭ on the fourth accidental button. The sequence involves more pushing and pulling than the right hand method. Pull the F on the C row; push the same for E; pull the D on the third; push for C; pull B♭ on the fourth accidental; push the same for A; pull the lowest note on the C row for G and finish with a pull on the lowest accidental for F.

Now practise the whole range which is three octaves—enough for any budding writer of fancy tunes! There is a complete octave available on the right-hand side but it gets a mite squeaky at the very top. It contains some difficult fingering patterns but follow *figures 24a* and *b* and unless being used to counter some bombard or Breton pipe music, then it is of little interest.

The chord patterns associated with the key of F major are easily played and do sound beautiful when well executed. *Figures 26a, b, c* and *d* on page 34 show the main chords for the scale.

TUNES IN F MAJOR

Page 35 shows ***The humours of Westport,*** a fine reel and generally played quite briskly but it is a difficult tune and some right hand help may be needed. In bar 6, all the notes except E are pulled. The sequence is shown in *figures 25a* and *b.* The tune can be heard on an old album by Matt Molloy, Tommy Peoples and Paul Brady called, inventively, 'Matt Molloy, Tommy Peoples and Paul Brady' and more recently on the Altan album 'Harvest Storm' (Green Linnet CSIF117).

From the original O'Neill's 'The Dance Music of Ireland: 1,001 Gems' there are only two reels, three jigs and one slip jig in the key of F major so that gives you some idea of its low popularity amongst the American-Irish fraternity at the turn of the 20th century. However, back on native turf, the key was well publicised in 'The Darley and McCall Collection' of just prior to world war one. A facsimile of this book was re-issued in 1984 by Ossian Publications - see *Appendix six.* Many of the airs are not memorable but the practise available is of clear value to the Anglo player in the Irish style and the odd useful air appears occasionally. This book also contains a smattering of D minor tunes.

The Shannon's flowery banks, again on page 35, is a sentimental song tune. It contains no B♭ but is still firmly and indisputably in the key of F major.

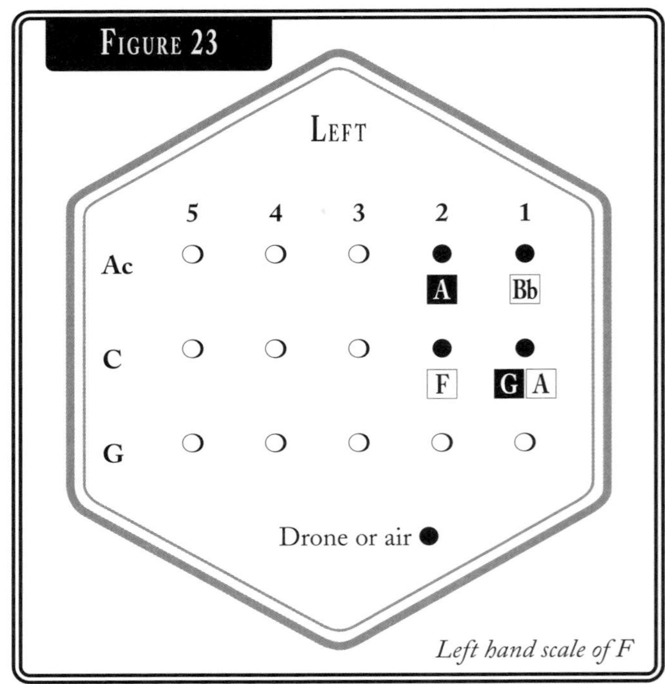

Left hand scale of F

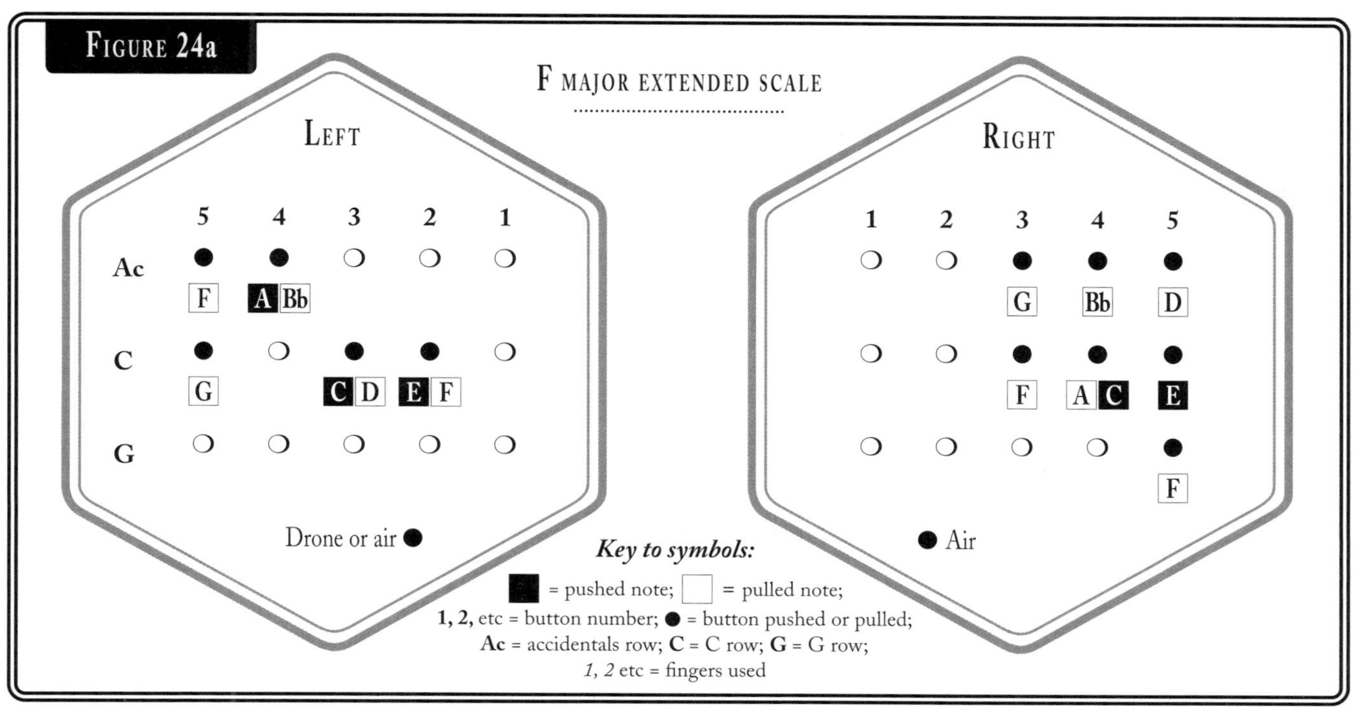
FIGURE 24a
F MAJOR EXTENDED SCALE
LEFT
5 4 3 2 1
Ac
F
A Bb
C
G
C D E F
G
Drone or air
RIGHT
1 2 3 4 5
G Bb D
F A C E
F
Air
Key to symbols:
= pushed note; = pulled note;
1, 2, etc = button number; ● = button pushed or pulled;
Ac = accidentals row; C = C row; G = G row;
1, 2 etc = fingers used

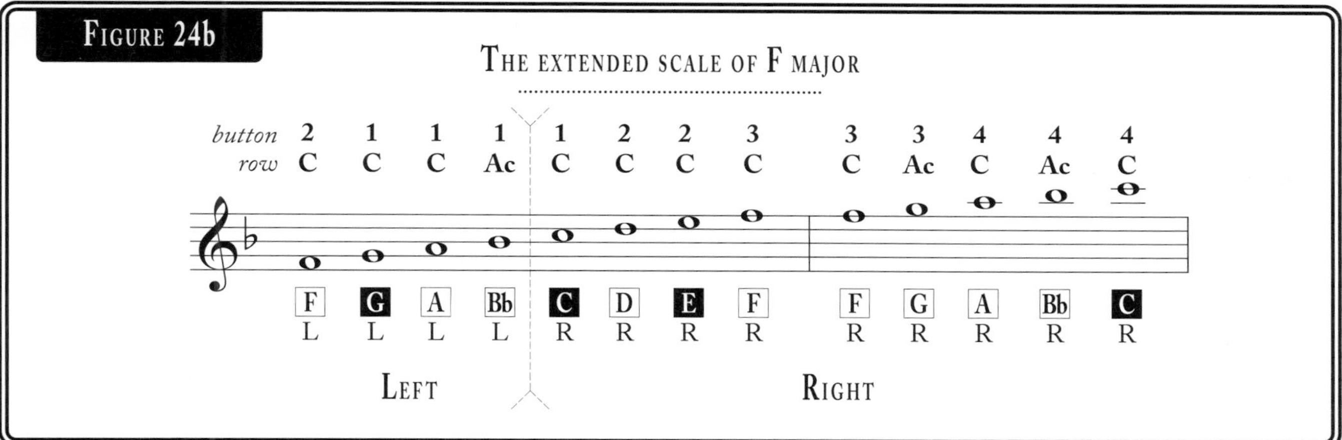
FIGURE 24b
THE EXTENDED SCALE OF F MAJOR
button 2 1 1 1 1 2 2 3 3 3 4 4 4
row C C C Ac C C C C C Ac C Ac C
F G A Bb C D E F F G A Bb C
L L L L R R R R R R R R R
LEFT
RIGHT

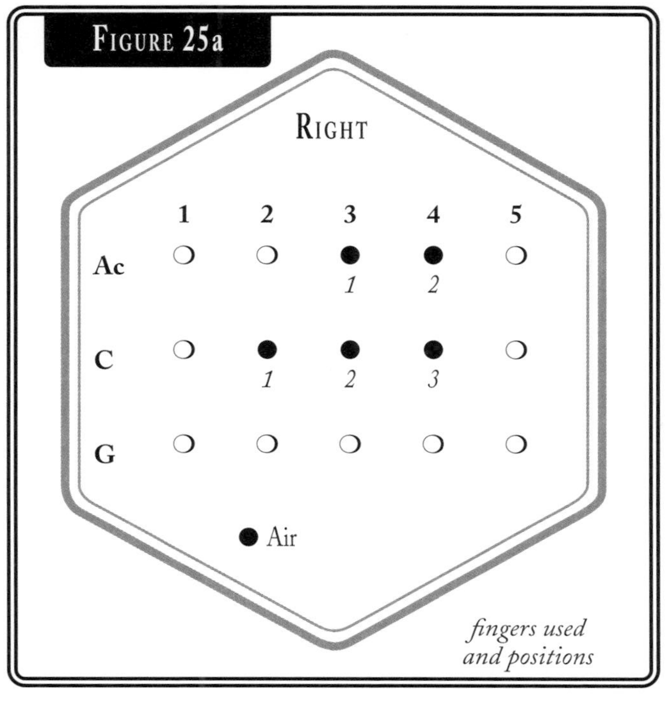
FIGURE 25a
RIGHT
1 2 3 4 5
Ac
1 2
C
1 2 3
G
Air
fingers used
and positions

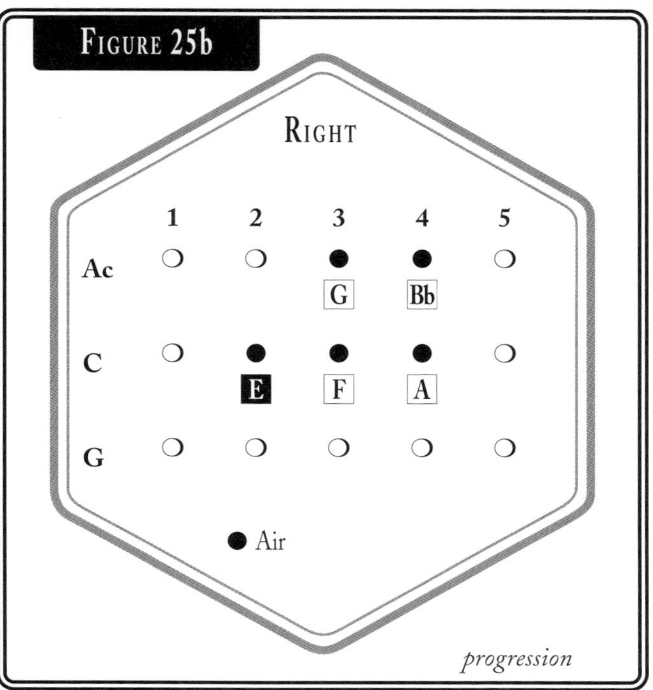
FIGURE 25b
RIGHT
1 2 3 4 5
Ac
G Bb
C
E F A
G
Air
progression

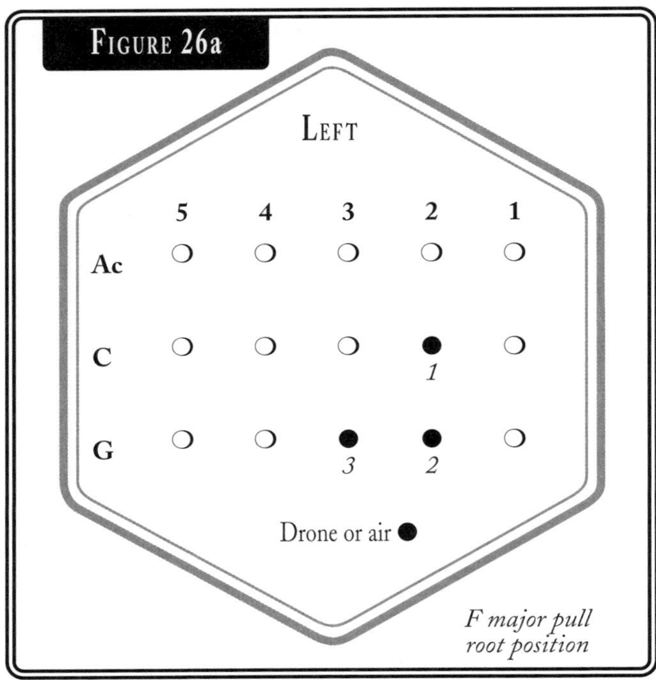

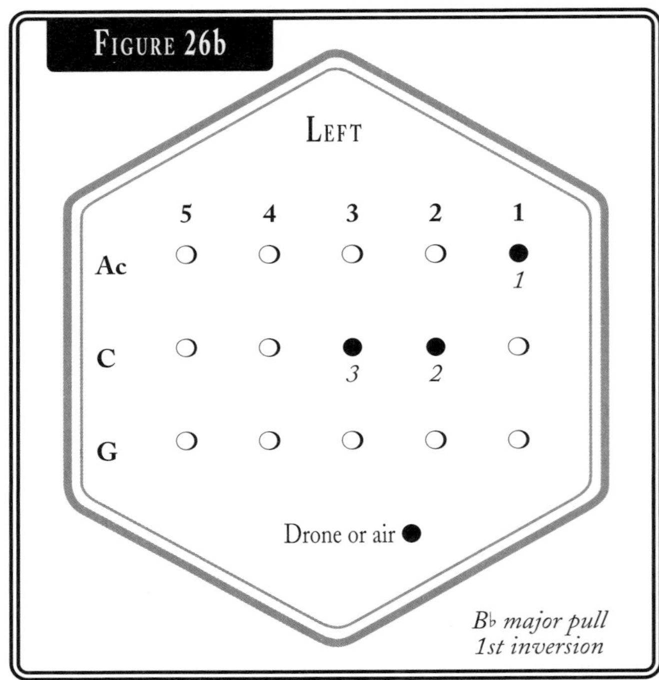

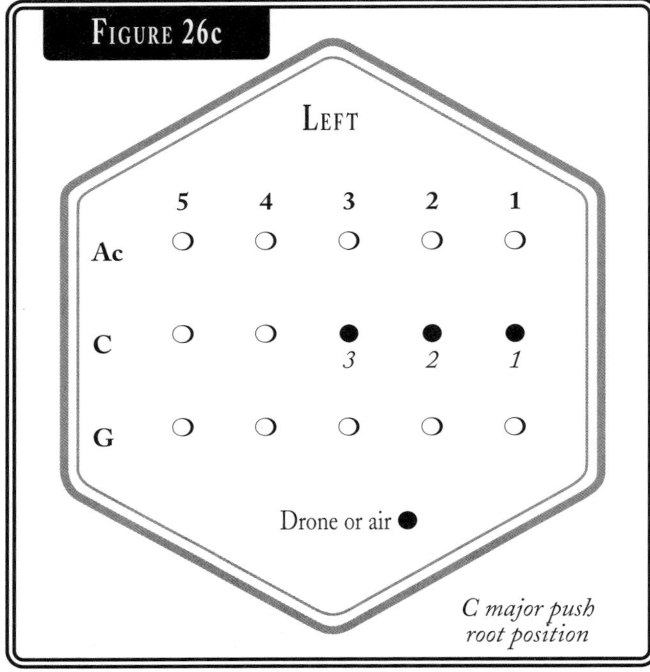

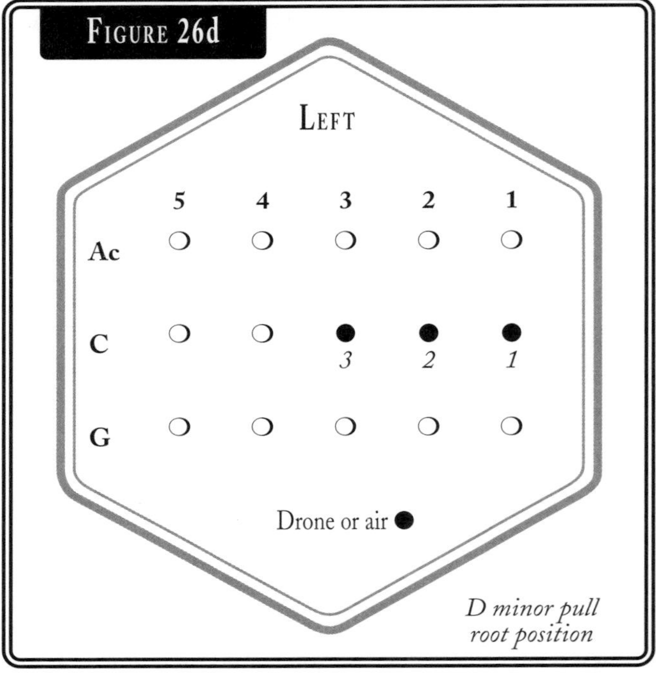

Key to symbols:
1, 2, etc = button number; ● = button pushed or pulled;
Ac = accidentals row; **C** = C row; **G** = G row;
1, 2 etc = fingers used

The humours of Westport

Track 17

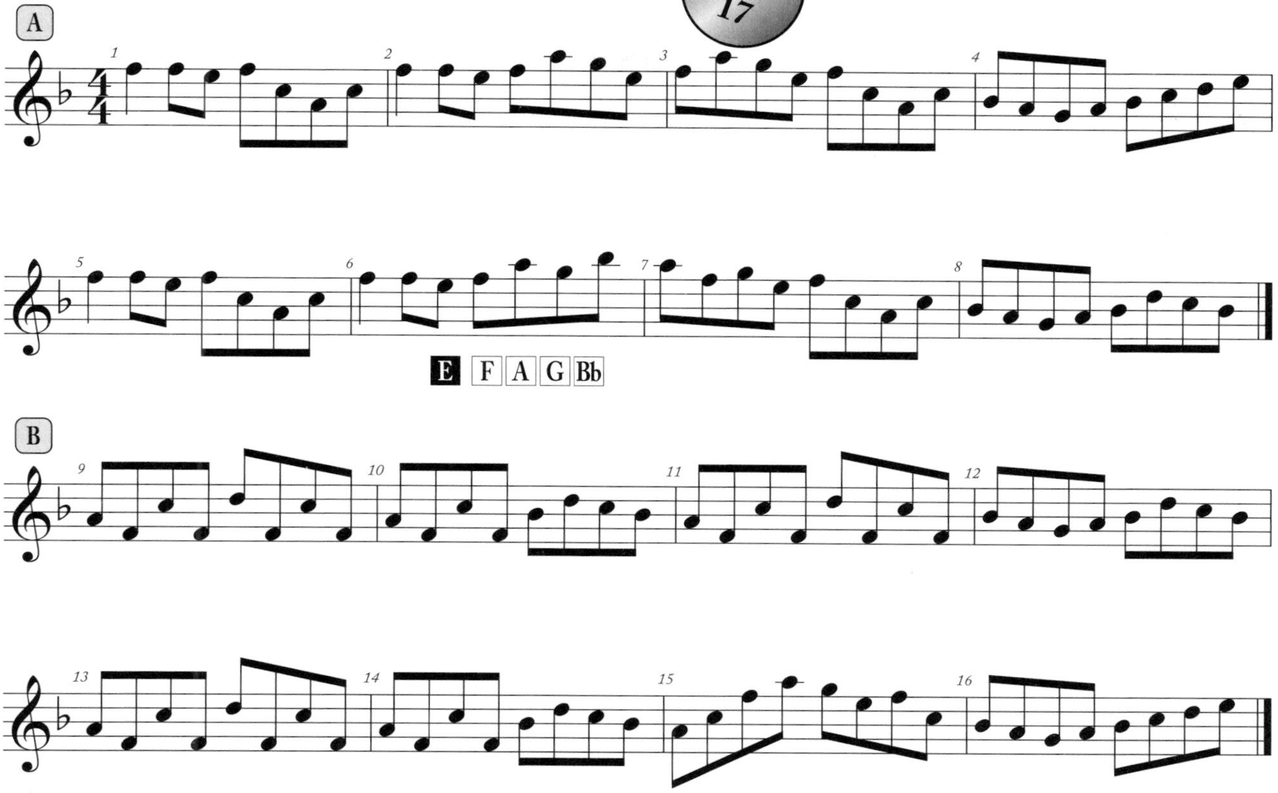

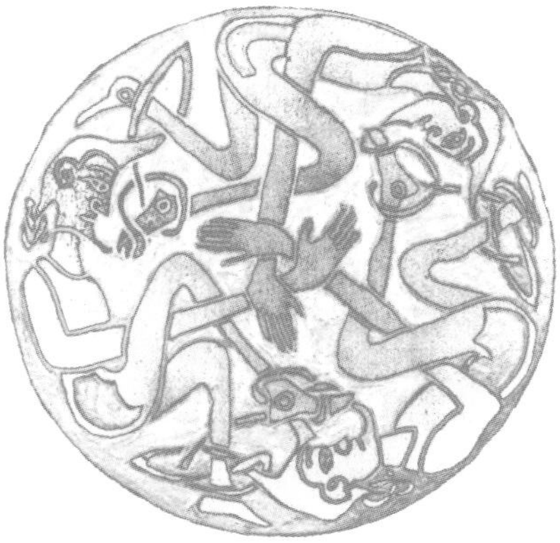

A

E F A G Bb

B

The key of B minor

B minor contains two sharpened notes—those of F♯ and C♯—and is therefore relative to D major. I have not discovered masses of music written in this key but the odd beauty pops up now and again and it is often used in modulation with D major. A knowledge of the key is thus essential.

The more accidentals that occur on the stave then the more difficult will become the fingering of the key. B minor is no exception and it requires a lot of concentration to achieve a smooth flow of any melody. An easy, non-extended scale falls nicely under the fingers of the right hand. Start with the first button on the C row and pull a B; pull a C♯ from the accidentals (first or second button); pull a D on the C row; push the same for E; now onto the G row and pull the F♯; push the same for G; pull the second button for A and push to complete the octave with a B. See *figure 28.*

There is a complete octave in the left-hand with but one accidental position to be played. It is shown opposite as *figure 30.* The run also ends with your fingers in good order to play a chord of B minor but again, that will depend on the notes available to you on the lower end of your Anglo. Start with B on the right-hand side; pull the A from the first button C row; push for G; pull the F♯ with the little finger from the G row (the only one over there usually); push E on the C row; pull the D below it; over to the accidental third button and push C♯; finish by pulling the fourth on the C row with a B. So, you have two complete octaves and all within a very mellow audible range. *Figure 29* shows the fingering for the rich chord of B minor pull to end your scale with a flourish.

Most tunes written in B minor or modulating into the key will occur in the lower octave range of the scale described. You will need the low A on the accidental fourth button in the left hand to achieve the tune on page 38, ***Martin Wynne's no. 2.*** Play it slowly. The range, two octaves and one tone, is wide and the intervals between the notes give it real flair.

In order to stay on top of the lessons so far, go back a couple of chapters and re-work the tunes from each section. It may have taken you a long time to get to this stage but do not forget what has gone before!

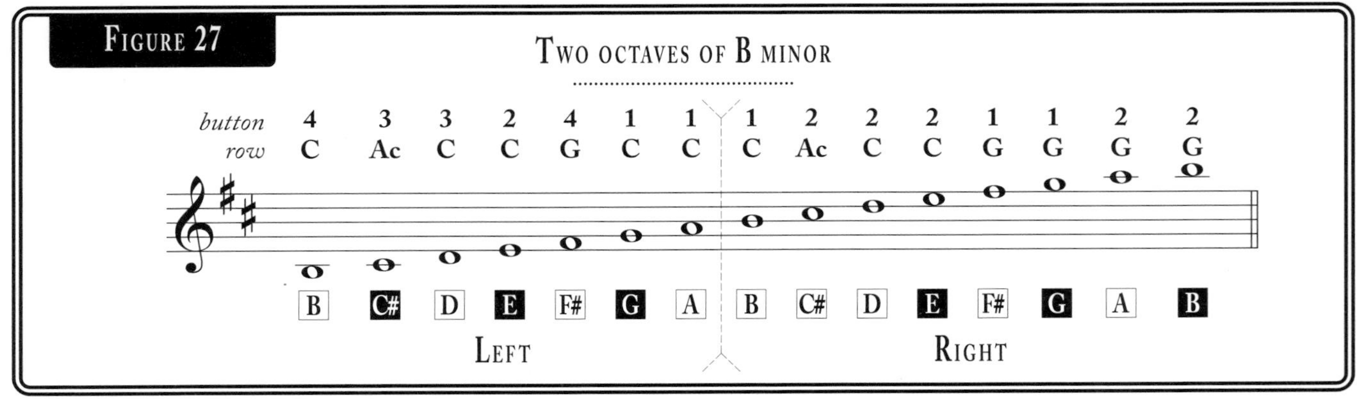

Figure 27

Two octaves of B minor

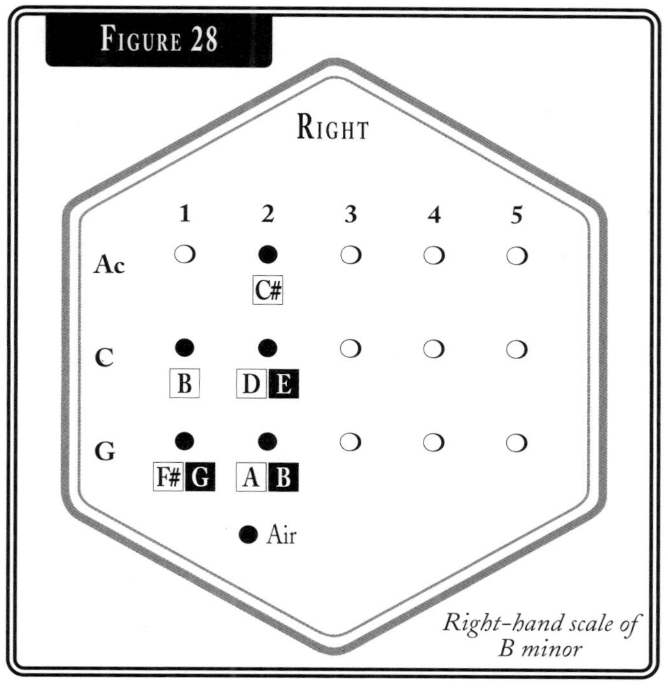

Right-hand scale of B minor

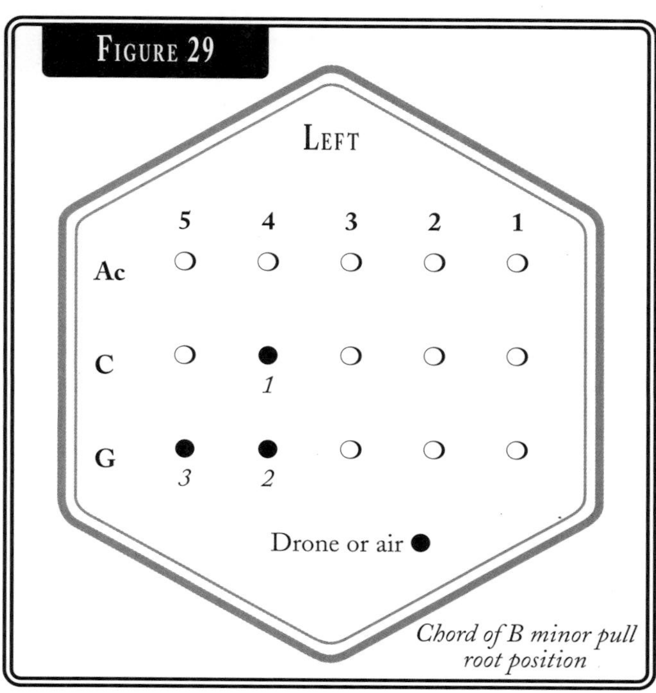

Chord of B minor pull root position

Key to symbols:

■ = pushed note; □ = pulled note;
1, 2, etc = button number; ● = button pushed or pulled;
Ac = accidentals row; **C** = C row; **G** = G row;
1, 2 etc = fingers used

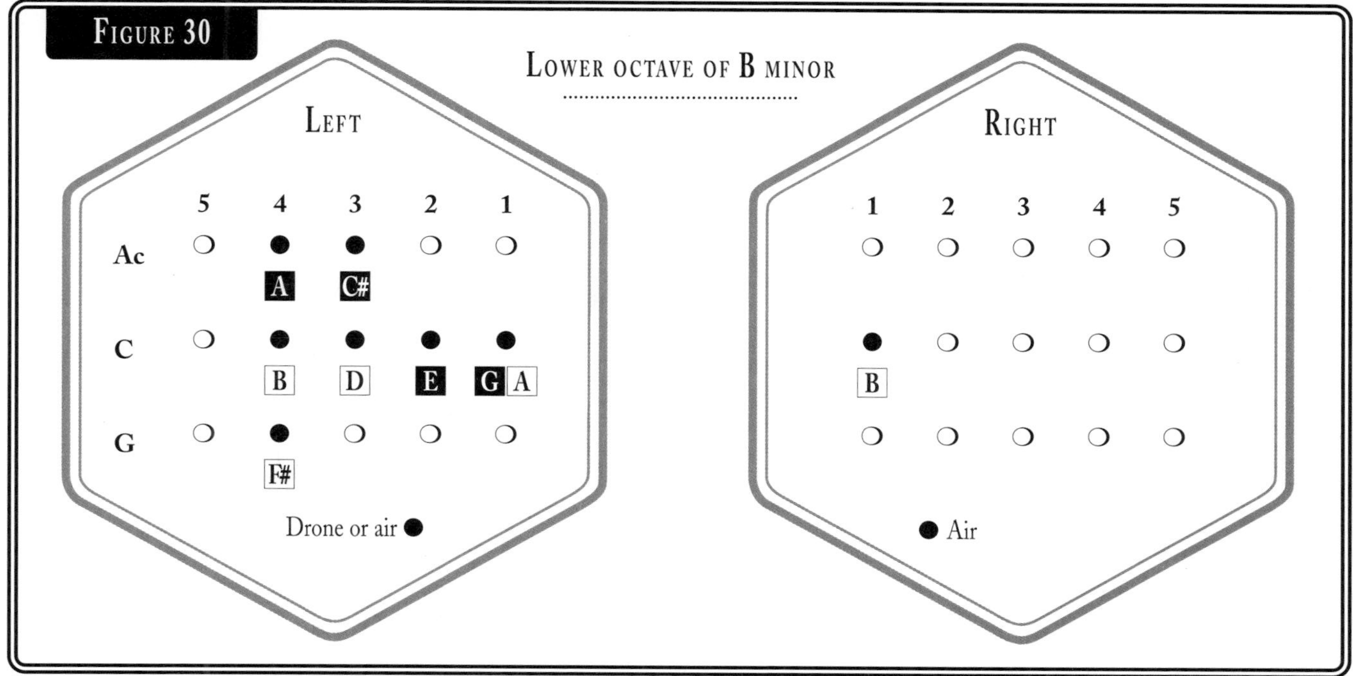

Martin Wynne's no. 2

Track 19

A

D B B D B A
L L L L L L

B

1. 2.

...And still further on

If you are not already a gibbering idiot with sunken, black-ringed eyes resulting from late night practise in the garden shed with only a candle to illuminate your dog-eared music, then this final analysis of possibilities should create the above image within a very short time.

It is not truly necessary to go beyond the scales and keys described thus far but they can be found; so why not have a crack? You may decide that any further contortions are not for you and that the basic keys are far enough along the trail for your immediate needs. It may be that you will stumble upon obscure key signatures quite by accident and will therefore gain greater satisfaction that way rather than by being given this guided tour through the maze.

Another important key that does occur regularly in music from the British Isles is that of A major. Scottish fiddle books are festooned with tunes in A and it is a good key for banjo and mandolin players. It has drawbacks on the concertina due to the presence of the three sharpened notes but try it for yourself and see how you fare. Happily, many tunes notionally in the key of A major avoid G♯.

THE KEY OF A MAJOR

The three sharps on the stave are F♯, C♯ and G♯, all available on your chromatic Anglo and two of them should be familiar to you by now. The newcomer is G♯ and it requires changes of direction in the bellows to use it on both sides.

The scale can be almost pulled from the box with the exception of the G♯ on the right-hand side. Start by pulling the A in the left hand (you should know where that is in your sleep); move to the B on the right-hand side and pull; pull the C♯ on the accidental row; pull D on the C row; push the same for E *or* pull it from the left-hand G row; pull F♯ on the right-hand G row; now push the G♯ which may be the third button on the accidental row and finish by pulling A from the right-hand C row.

There is a full octave in the left hand; it starts by pulling the A button on the C row. Push the first accidental to get G♯; little finger for the F♯; push E on the C row; pull the D out of the third button; push the C♯ accidental third; pull B on the fourth button C row and push the low A on the fourth accidental. See *figure 33a.* Practise this sequence for a long time. It is difficult and the wrong buttons can create some evil sounds. There is a nice, full chord on the left-hand side which can be made with a push: see *figure 33b.*

On page 41 are two tunes which explore A major: ***The humours of Ballycastle*** and ***Oh, the britches full of stitches.*** Please, take them steadily as they are full of potholes for the unwary. There is a recurring theme in many A major tunes and it can be found in bars 2, 6 and 14 of ***The humours of Ballycastle.*** The fingering is very easy and it is worthwhile learning it if only as a decorative passage to add to other melodies. See *figure 34.* A similar motif occurs in reels in A major. The sequence is better described as follows: all the notes are pushed starting with C♯ on either of the first or second accidental in the right hand; push the accidental row A in the left; push E on the right-hand C row and go back to A on the left. You will begin to recognise it in all sorts of keys as you become more aware of the structure of traditional music.

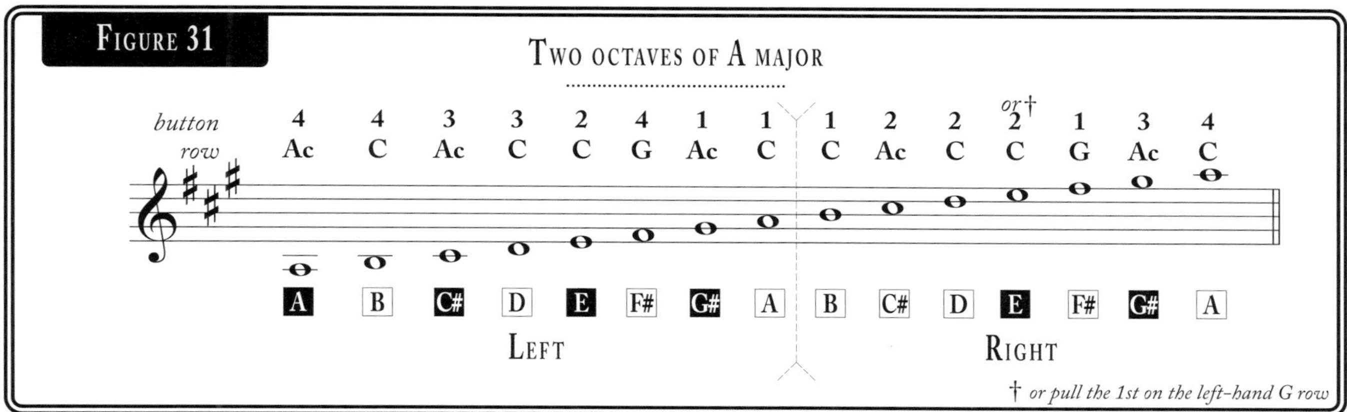

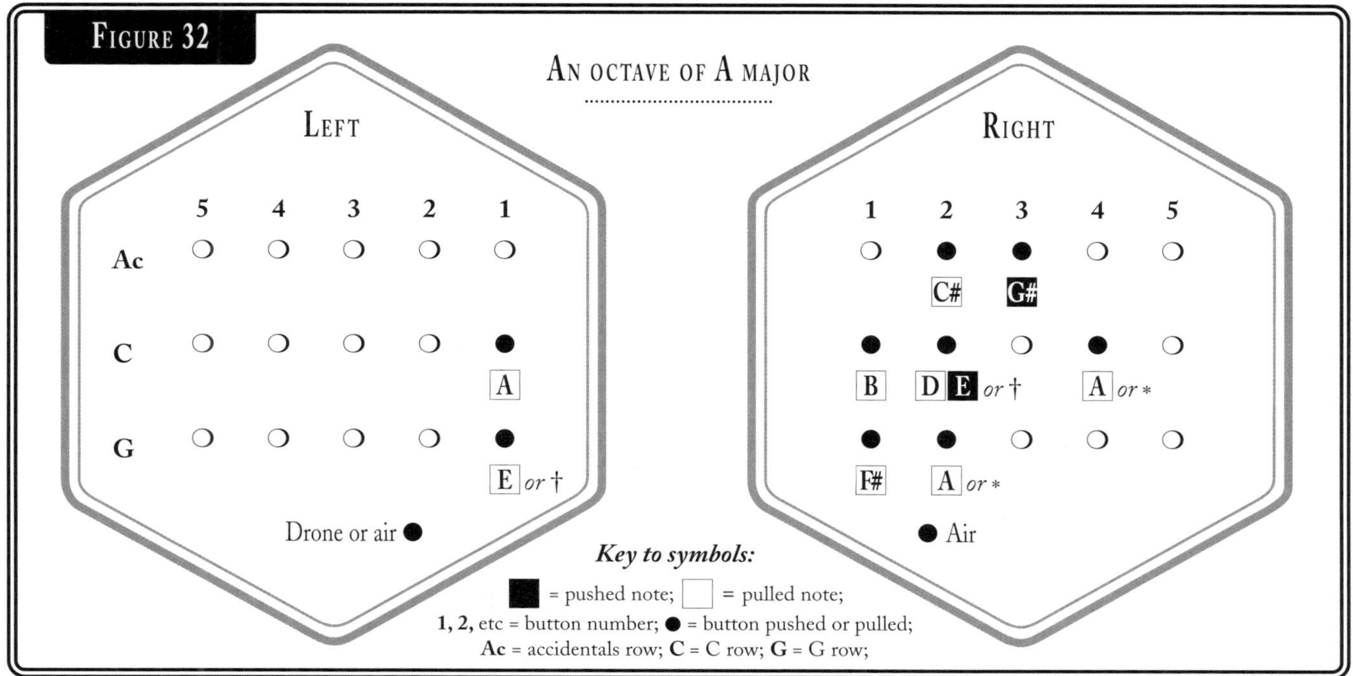

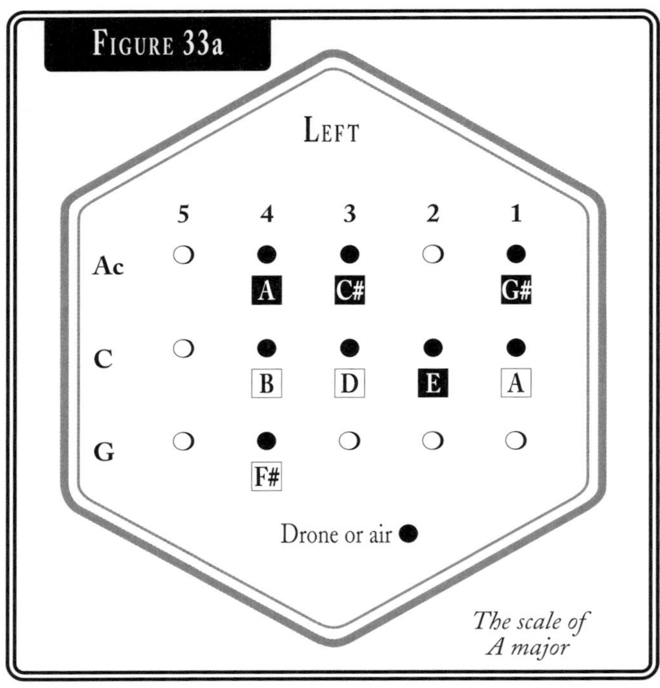

The scale of A major

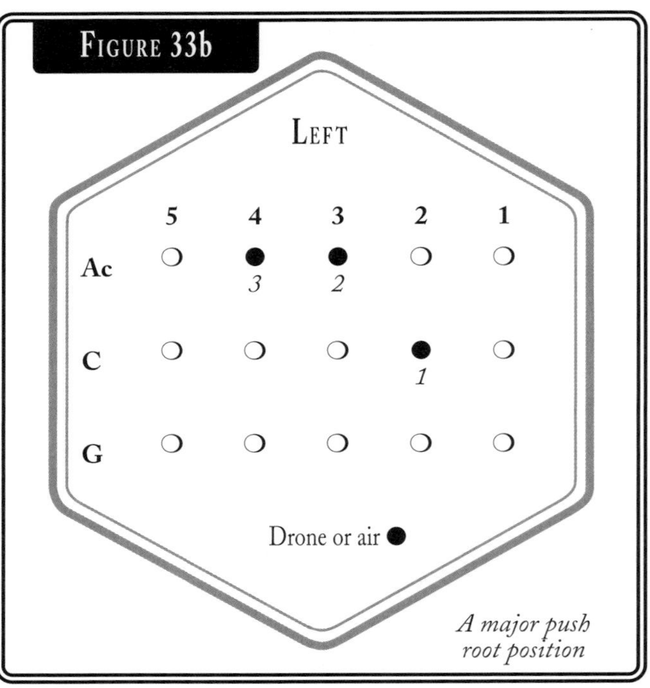

A major push root position

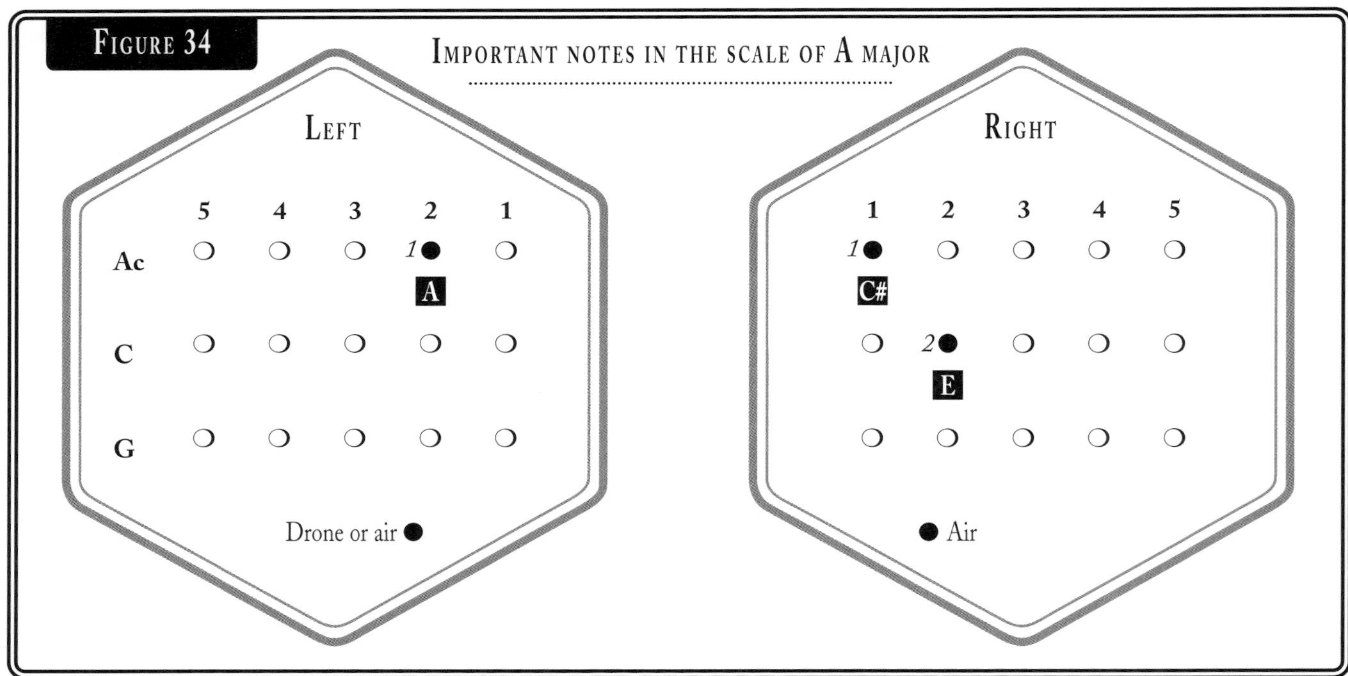

Key to symbols:

■ = pushed note; □ = pulled note;
1, 2, etc = button number; ● = button pushed or pulled;
Ac = accidentals row; **C** = C row; **G** = G row;
1, 2 etc = fingers used

The humours of Ballycastle

Oh, the britches full of stitches

The key of G minor

The key of G minor is well known to fiddle players and to those who play on the chromatic button accordeon in the B and C configuration. It has a plaintive scale which lends itself well to slow airs and laments, both of these forms being suitable for performance on the Anglo.

The scale contains two flats and is relative to B flat major, one of those keys to avoid on your concertina. All the flat notes occur on the third, accidental row and in a variety of push-pull situations. We have already used B♭ but E♭ is a new problem to tackle. It is usually found on the first two buttons on the right-hand side and on the third button down on the left as a pulled note. Consult your chart of notes in order to sort out your own system, although there is a strong chance that it will concur with mine. The chord of G minor is easy to play either as a standard tonic triad or as an inversion. *Figures 35a* and *b* show the two varieties of chord with their finger positions.

Figure 36 gives you the scale. You can, alternatively, use the C row pushed G as a starting point and then pull the A on the first button. Pull B♭ on the accidental row; push C on the right; pull D; pull E♭ from either the first or second accidental; pull F and push for the octave G. As usual, practise the scale until it becomes smooth.

Extension above the octave is easy enough and a full octave below is available on the left-hand side. *Figure 37* may be easier to follow than words for this difficult key. When, indeed *if*, you feel comfortable with this key, then try the tune given on page 44, ***Carolan's welcome;*** also, see if you can find others from printed sources or recordings. For instance, there is a nice enough slip jig in G minor with the intriguing title of 'The night before Larry was stretched' which, believe me, will stretch your capabilities. It was coupled with another eccentrically named but tuneful slip jig 'Quick! we have but a second' and recorded on a little-known, truly excellent album entitled 'The Fort of Kincora' by the Clare button accordeonist Martin Connolly, accompanied on piano by Maureen Glyn, under Martin's own label and catalogue number MCMG1. Another popular tune in this key is 'Dowd's favourite' but the second part unfortunately modulates into B♭ and is a challenge for any instrument. Nonetheless, it is a cracking tune and well worth seeking out.

There are many tunes—airs, reels, jigs and hornpipes—which utilise the *mixolydian* mode; that is, the seventh of the scale is flattened. A great number of these are in the key of G and some occasionally have a flattened B, often as a passing note. You will find that modes can be combined within a tune and so your fingering systems will need to be fluid and interchangeable. Take 'The girl who broke my heart' as an example; it is shown as the first reel in O'Neill's.

I feel that you have enough to be getting on with for now and do not intend to reach deeper into the more obscure scales. As I have already intimated, those scales will only be encountered in 'composed' pieces and if you become proficient and confident, then they will begin to fall under your fingers without me having to show you how.

At which juncture, there is little left to say about the method apart from the use of decoration. This is a complicated field and is open to much personal interpretation though a modicum of assistance would probably be useful.

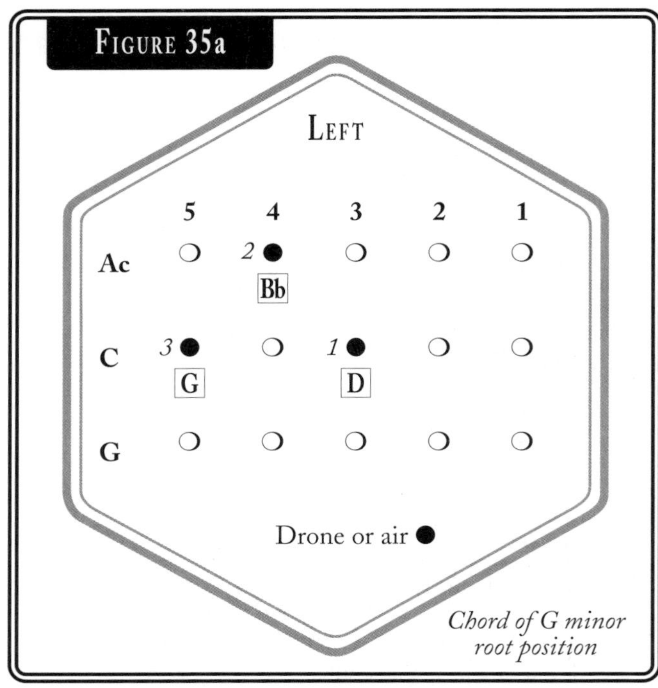

Chord of G minor root position

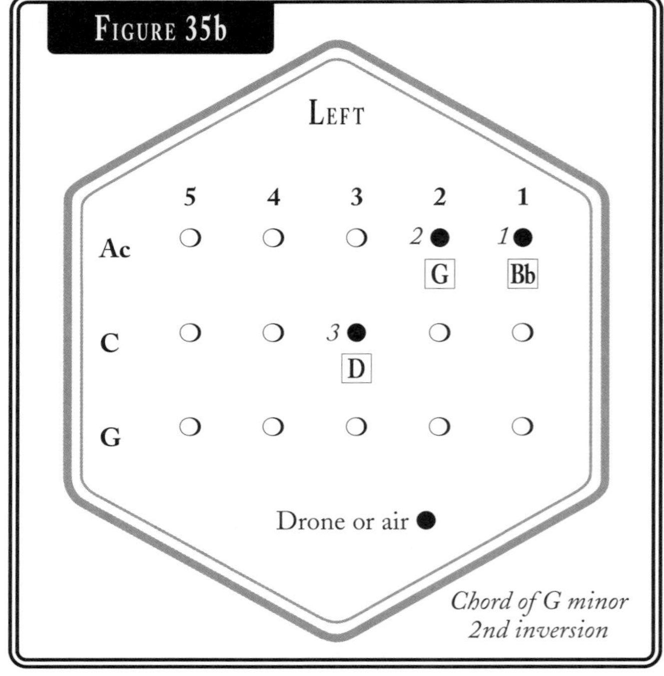

Chord of G minor 2nd inversion

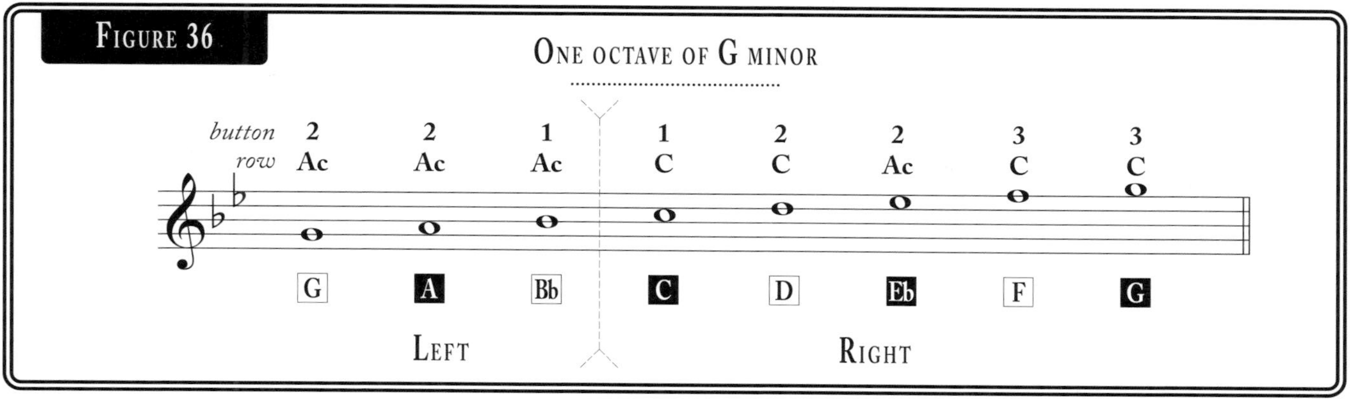

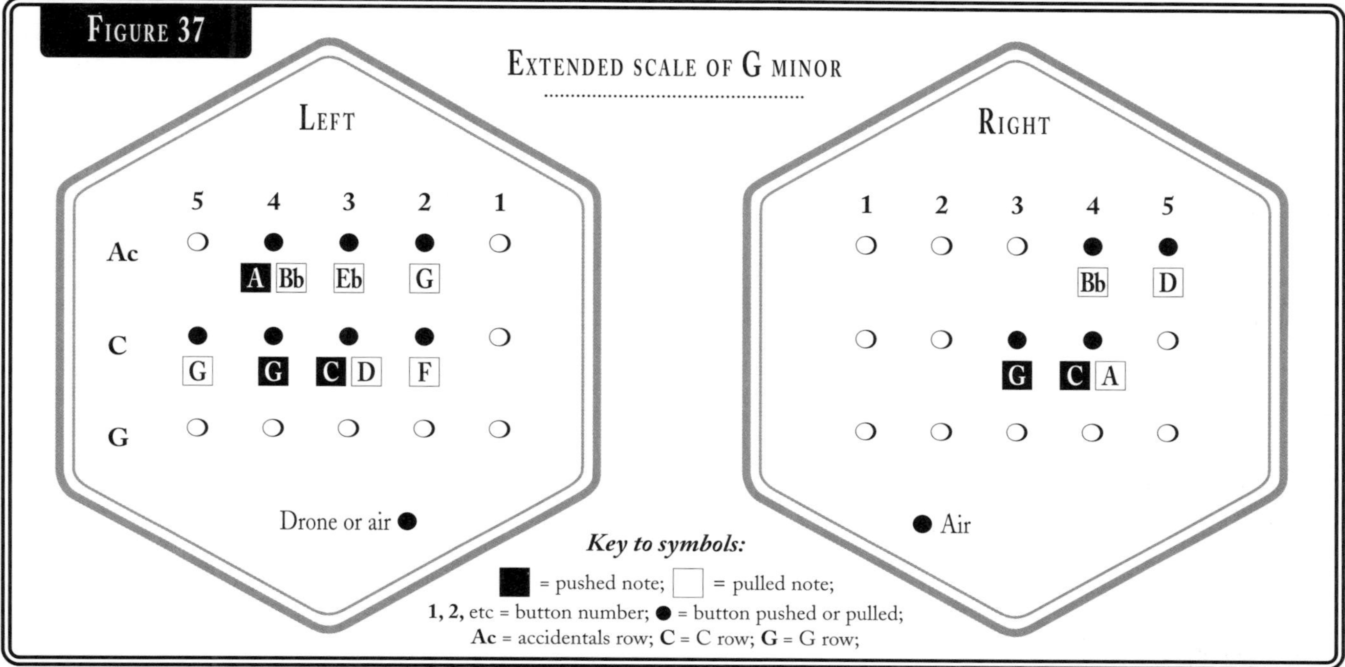

The Anglo concertina in its own environment, the kitchen of an Irish family home. House céilís are still common in many parts of Ireland and can be found increasingly in England as the pleasure of set dancing spreads throughout the country

Carolan's welcome

Track 22

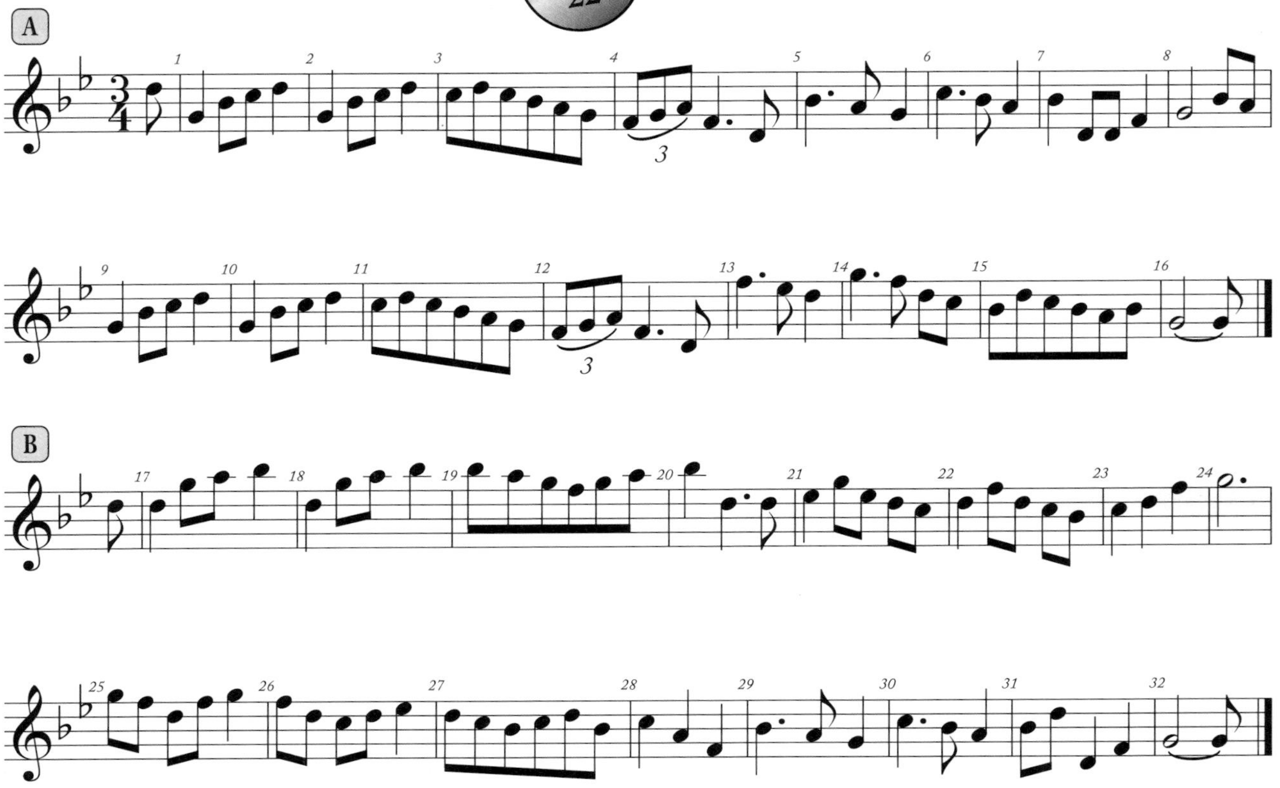

A

B

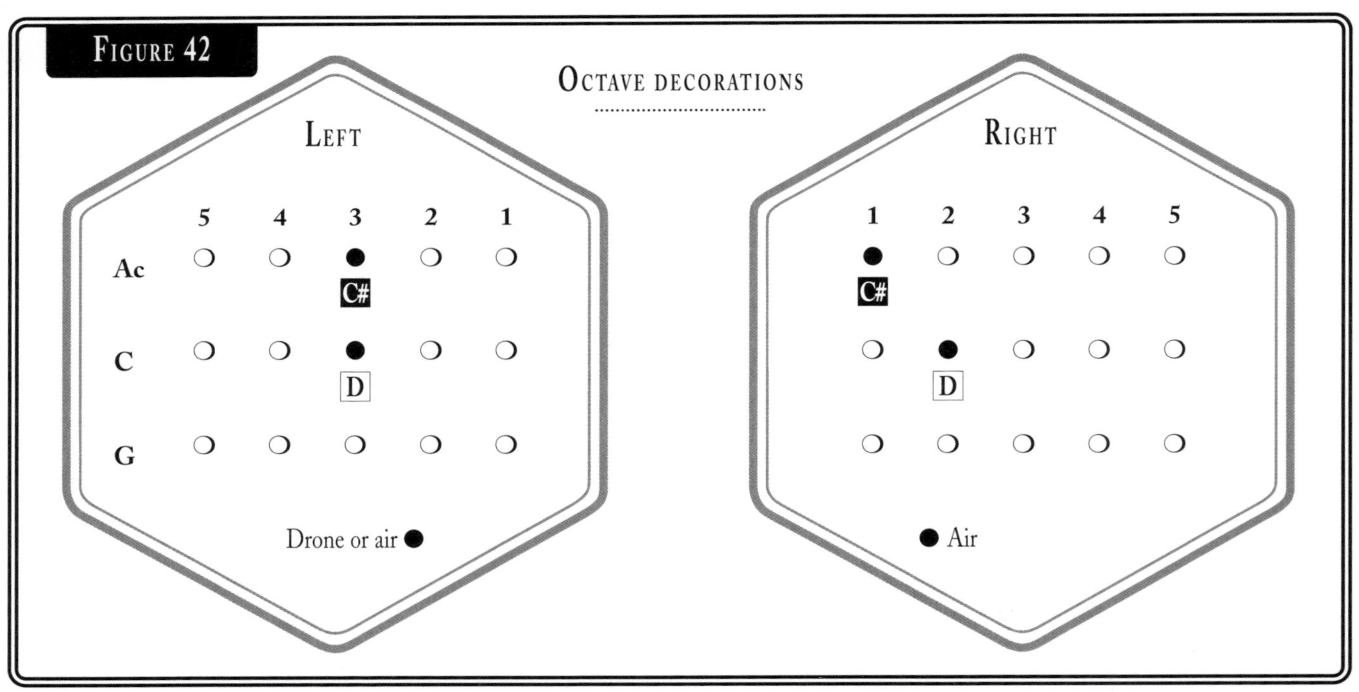

Key to symbols:

■ = pushed note; □ = pulled note;
1, 2, etc = button number; ● = button pushed or pulled;
Ac = accidentals row; **C** = C row; **G** = G row;

DECORATION OF MELODIC LINES

I suppose the most common form of decoration known to traditional musicians is the triplet in either jig ($\frac{6}{8}$) time or reel ($\frac{4}{4}$) time. It is played relatively simply on the violin and, due to the large size of the buttons, it can be achieved well on the melodeon or button accordeon. Our little gadget is somewhat less amenable when it comes to decoration. I intend to show a method which has its roots in early and Renaissance music and is used by composers to this day to describe elements of decoration.

Firstly examine *figure 38,* a line of a hornpipe rich in triplets. Let us determine whether it is possible to play it as written.

FIGURE 38

As you will find, it can be played in the first method, by pushing and pulling the melody line out of the box. Hornpipes are often played at a leisurely pace by revival musicians but this was not always the case. In the Irish piping tradition, the form was played rather like a dotted reel and set dancers still like the tempo very fast for hornpipe figures.

In *figure 39,* the examples of jigs, the notes in the triplets are almost twice the speed of the quavers which make up the bulk of the melody in most ($\frac{6}{8}$) tunes. Try playing the lines slowly so that the semi-quavers do sound faster.

FIGURE 39

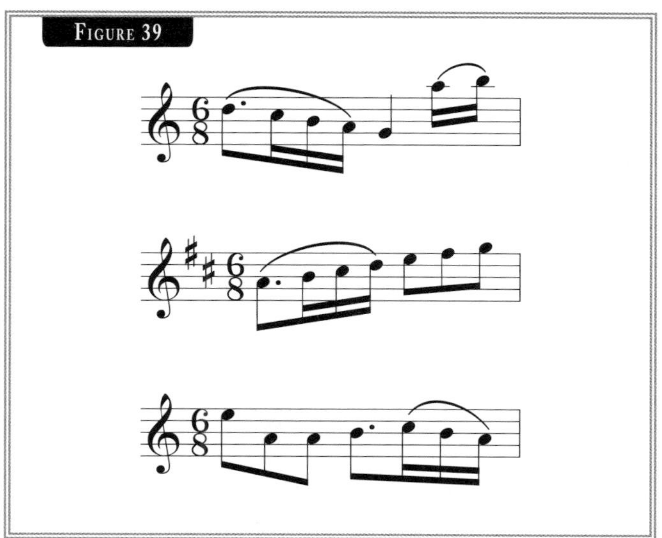

You will find a mixture of pull and pull-push will increase the fluidity of the melody as you get better at it. Reels tend to make novice players cringe but once you have the systematic approach of this method at your fingertips, they do become easier—with time!

The reel in G in *figure 40* can be approached from two angles. The first bar is very much a pull-push tune using the first method described in this tutor. The second bar however, is more in line with the second method for G where the notes are pulled out. The difference in fluidity is very noticeable and the bar flows freely, without the staccato associated with the previous bar.

FIGURE 40

The reel in D *(figure 41,* below) is of the type that concertina players find the most difficult to come to terms with; a straight triplet on one note. As a generalisation, the note has to be pulled or pushed.

FIGURE 41

Trying to play the note on one button does create a staccato effect. I adopt a system which involves the inclusion of an octave to the written note *(figure 42* opposite shows the location, *figure 43a,* below, the notation) or a mordent, *(figures 43b* and *43c)* either above or below the note.

There are a few places where straight triplets can be played on two buttons such as G or A in the left hand, G or A in the right hand and a difficult B in the right and left hand. The device of using an octave is my favourite and is quite acceptable when trying to achieve rapidity in melodic passages.

FIGURE 43

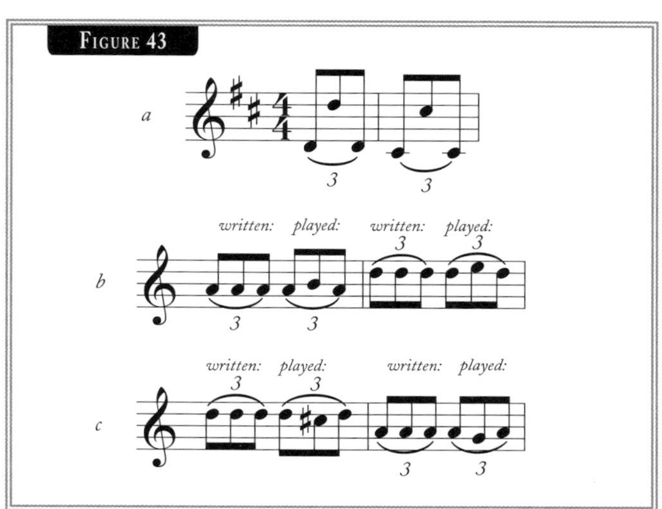

Naturally enough, one cannot slide between notes on the concertina because of the mechanical way in which the sounds are formed. There is a decorative way round the problem of sliding however and it simply requires the use of totally chromatic sections added into the melodic sequence.

For example, instead of playing a run of notes as shown in *figure 44,* try including all or some of the notes in-between, such as the F natural, in the same passage, as demonstrated in *figure 45.* It is a grace note, not in the written key signature, but it adds character and quirkiness to the tune.

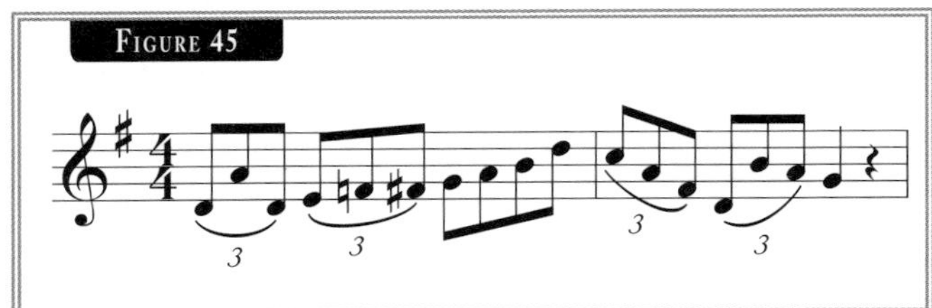

The trill or shake, written ***tr*** above a piece of music, is a rapid alternation of the written note and the one above it. It can be shown on the stave in two ways as in *figure 46.* It is little more than an upper or inverted mordant which has been stretched out to the limit. It is difficult to execute on the concertina and should be treated as a triplet in most cases.

Next, try out the hornpipe shown below, ***The flowing tide.*** It displays the inclusion of grace notes and triplets as means of decorating the melody.

Much of the decoration that pertains to traditional music will come to you with practise. Go back once more and see if you can add decorative motifs to the tunes accompanying each lesson. Constant revision means clearer understanding and, ultimately, better playing technique. Be adventurous: endeavour to find alternative places and intervals to play straight triplets and add a new dimension to your individual technique. Drop onto the accidental row and experiment while playing at speed; you will either find a splendid possibility or make such a discordant row that you will have to drop out of the melody line and come back in when you have recovered your equilibrium!

The flowing tide

The slow air

Slow airs, more than any other form in traditional music, conjure up the bleakness of landscape, the longing for lost hope and memories of days gone by. The Anglo concertina, with its single note voice, can give vent to such feelings as well as any other instrument.

The techniques described earlier are adequately suited to this type of tune. ***Her mantle so green,*** shown below, is a song tune and it is available on a Topic album re-issued in 1994 (Topic TS474), sung by Margaret Barry, the itinerant Irish singer. In the 1970s, I first heard it given the treatment as an air by Jackie Daly. The transcription only gives the bare bones of the tune. Decoration, lengthening and shortening of note values and pauses all give extra weight to the obvious yearning contained in the air.

Recordings of airs and laments are more common nowadays and you should listen to, for example, fiddlers such as Paddy Glackin, Seán Keane and the great Irish-American musician, Andy McGann. Matt Cranitch, who used to play with Na Filí, has recorded a whole album of slow airs. Flute players who can put across haunting airs are Cathal McConnell, Matt Molloy and the late Frankie Kennedy. Of the button accordeon players, Séamus Ó Beaglaoich, Jackie Daly and the phenomenal Sharon Shannon can all lay claim to be superior exponents of the lament.

Transcription of slow airs is often more difficult than other forms due to the idiosyncrasies of timing and phrasing with which it is so often associated. You will just have to listen much harder before you venture along this particular road. Virtually all slow airs are actually songs minus words; it is accepted that players should try, within the scope of their chosen instruments, to emulate the way in which a singer would interpret the song. Listen to recordings of the *sean-nós* tradition to gain insight; you don't necessarily have to understand the words to capture the feeling.

The dear Irish boy, shown overleaf, is a real tear jerker. It is difficult in that it has a great number of note values within it, from semi-quavers up to dotted minims. I suppose it is really open to interpretation by the individual player. A version of it can be heard by the piper, Felix Doran, on 'The Last of the Travelling Pipers' (Ossian, OSS63). The air is filled with triplets and trills and yet there is still room for 'personalising' the melody and making it your own.

Her mantle so green

Track 24

The dear Irish boy

Conclusion and Acknowledgments

The method contained in this tutor cannot be summarised rapidly or there would have been no need to write it all down in the first place! As I stressed at the outset, it is a system and systems are supposed to help us develop new ways of analysing and solving diffculties. The appendix (page 50 onwards) of tunes are just a few of my favourites on the Anglo and come from a wide range of sources both traditionally transmitted and from the printing press. The mix of tried and trusted chestnuts throughout the text, from band repertory and sessions in England and Ireland will, I hope, convince you that the method is suitable for all kinds of music, whatever its ethnic origin.

If you encounter any major pitfalls, I would be only too happy to help you out, if I can; any enquiries should be made through the publishers. Please enjoy the music and it would be great to go into a session somewhere, some time in the future and overhear a fine concertina player telling his listeners that he learned his method from this, my humble little book.

My initial thanks must go to Pete Coe of Ripponden, West Yorkshire, for encouraging me to start on this tutor in the first instance. It was Pete who also made contact with the publishers on my behalf and convinced them that there was a need for such a book.

To name individuals who have been influential throughout my long association with traditional music would require another volume and so, suffice to say, thank you to everyone that I know and have played music with for the past thirty years. A special thank you to Tim Lyons of Roscam, County Galway, for teaching me so many fine tunes. The first man that I saw playing Irish music on the concertina was Jackie Daly of Kanturk, County Cork and I am indebted to him for planting the seed and providing many grand melodies.

To Linda Bramich, who needed no introduction to the skill of proof reading, or to my idiosyncrasies with the pen, double thanks for putting up with me when practising the sacred art in numerous Irish bars whilst we should have really been on holiday.

The source of many fine sessions on the west coast of Ireland are the sailing boat festivals at Kinvarra, Spiddal and Ballyvaughan. This Irish hooker (húicéar in Irish) is moored at Ballyvaughan, County Clare, quay. It has been decked out whereas the older tradition was of open boats. They were used principally for supplying the Aran Islands with turf for the fire

Appendix One

A selection of favourite airs for the Anglo concertina

The selection of tunes contained here reflects only my own, perhaps narrow choice of music that is well suited to the concertina. You can scour all the collections ever printed and still manage to miss the odd gem and so I do not claim that this selection is complete in any way but simply some of the tunes that I find rewarding to play.

The transcriptions of traditional music have been gathered over a period of many years, most of them from 'session' tapes, from musicians not known to me by name. Any errors are down to me!

Trying to get tunes from recordings is a painfully acquired skill but is rewarding for the twists and turns with which skilled artistes can delight you. Don't think it's a gift to be born with: you simply have to persevere—learning by ear *can* be done, albeit slowly in most cases. After a couple of years trying, you might surprise yourself...

Shandon bells — D major

Track 27

A
D G A7 Em G
D G A7 G A7 G G
1. 2.
tr
B
D D A7 A7
Bm F♯m G A7 D
D.C.

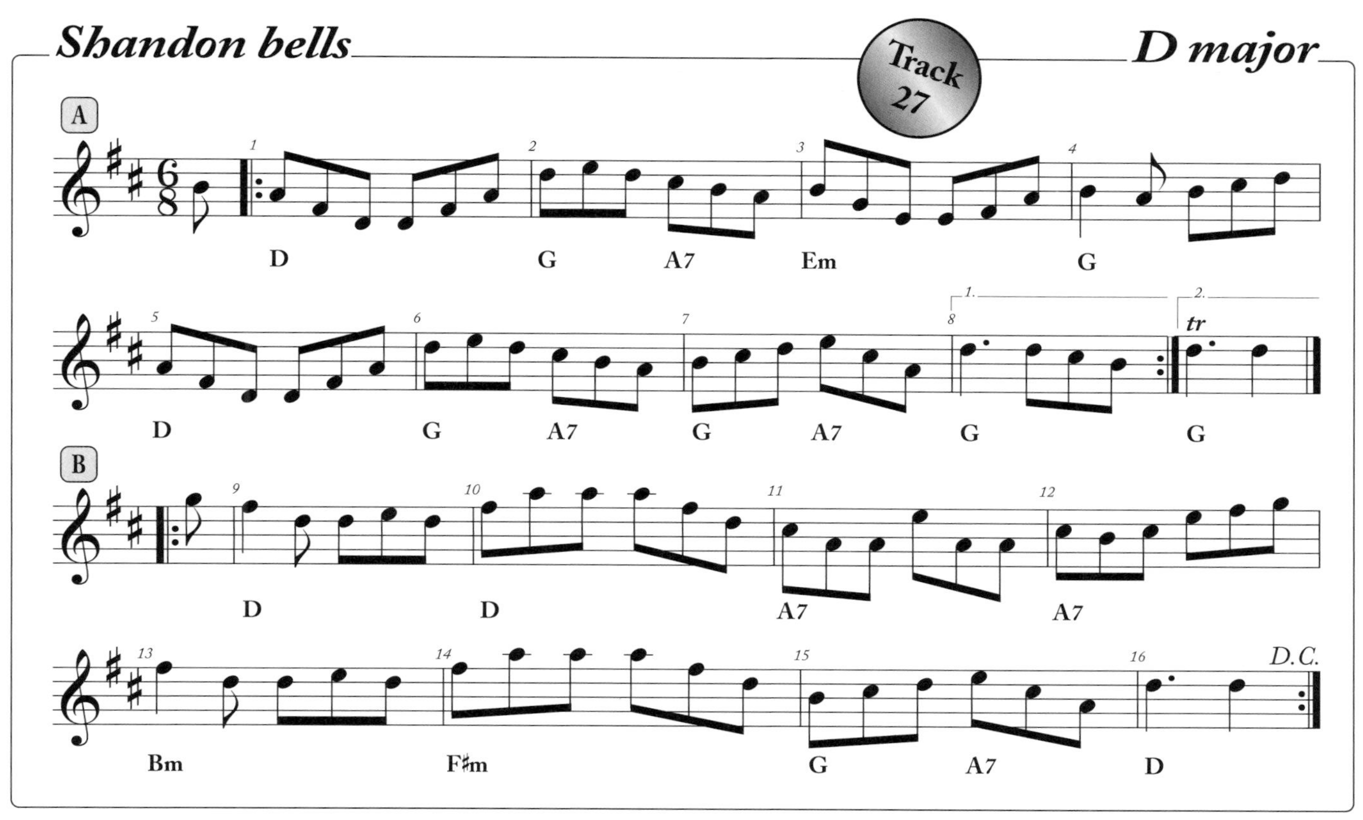

The pipe on the hob no. 1 — D modal

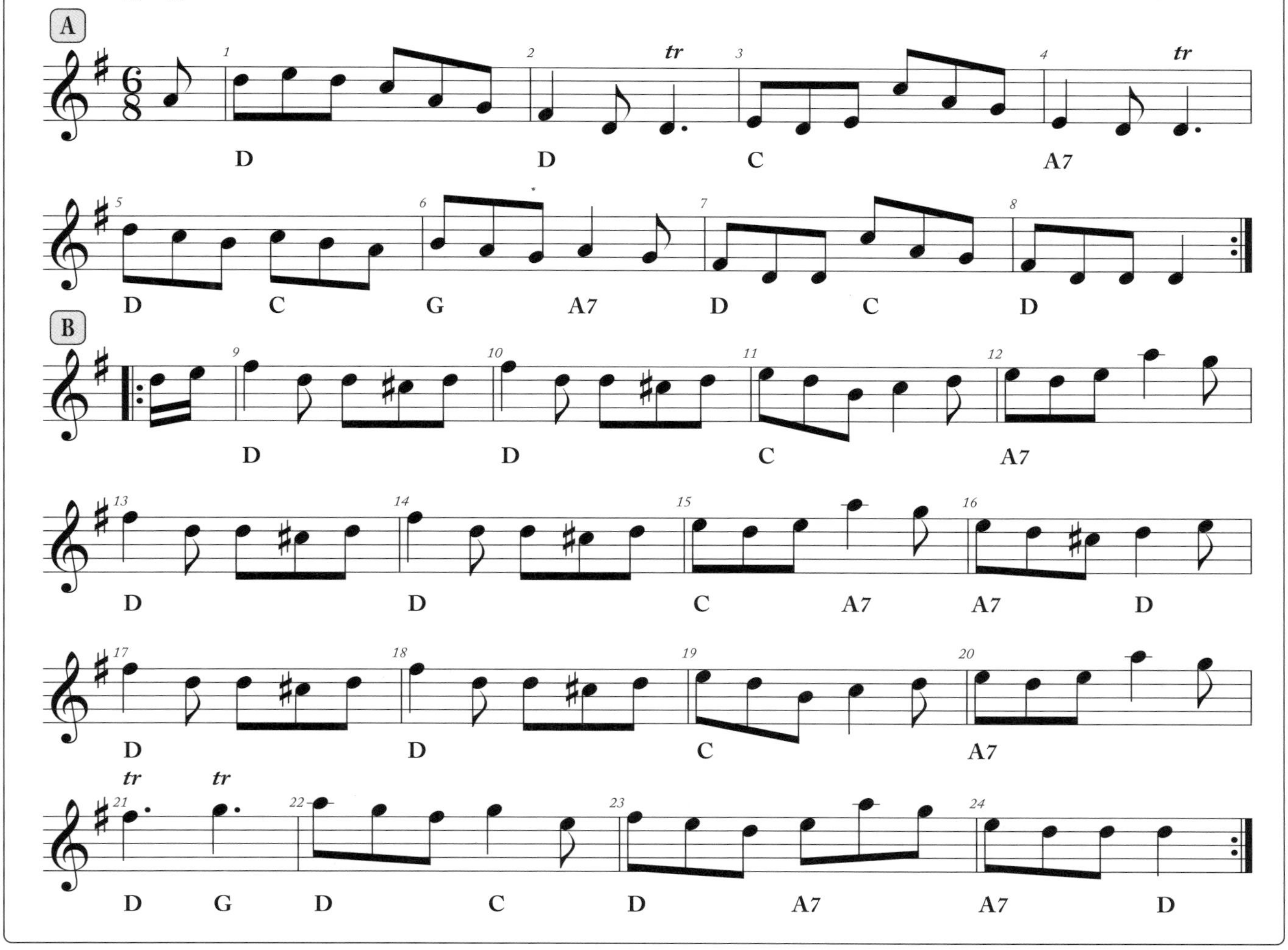

A
tr tr
D D C A7
D C G A7 D C D
B
D D C A7
D D C A7 A7 D
D D C A7
tr tr
D G D C D A7 A7 D

The cliffs of Moher — *A minor*

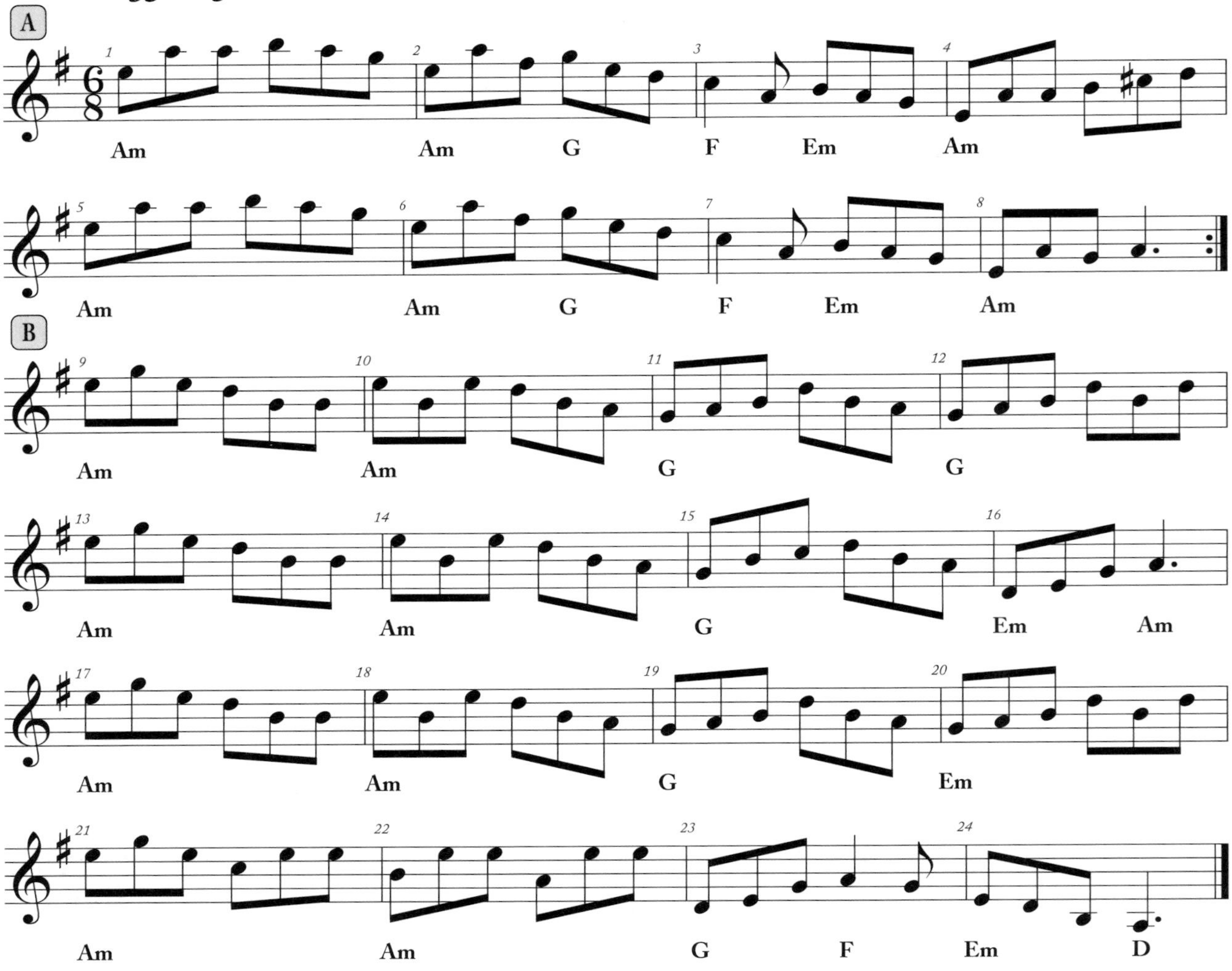
A
Am Am G F Em Am
Am Am G F Em Am
B
Am Am G G
Am Am G Em Am
Am Am G Em
Am Am G F Em D

I ne'er shall wean her — *A minor*

A
C C F Am
C C F F Em Am
B
C C Em Am Am F
C C F F Em Am

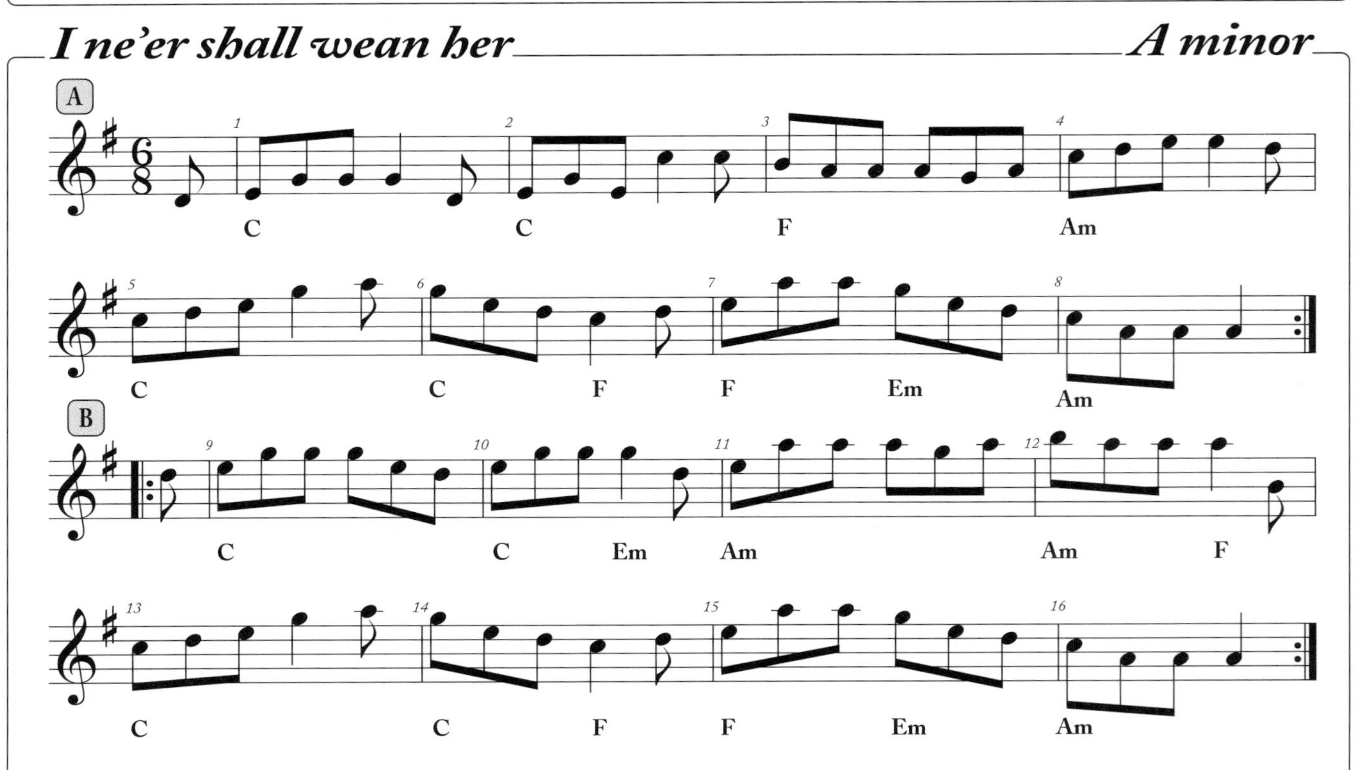

The eavesdropper — Track 26 — *G major*

A
G G C G A7 D
G G C A7 D G
B
G D C G C G A7 D
G D C G C A7 D G

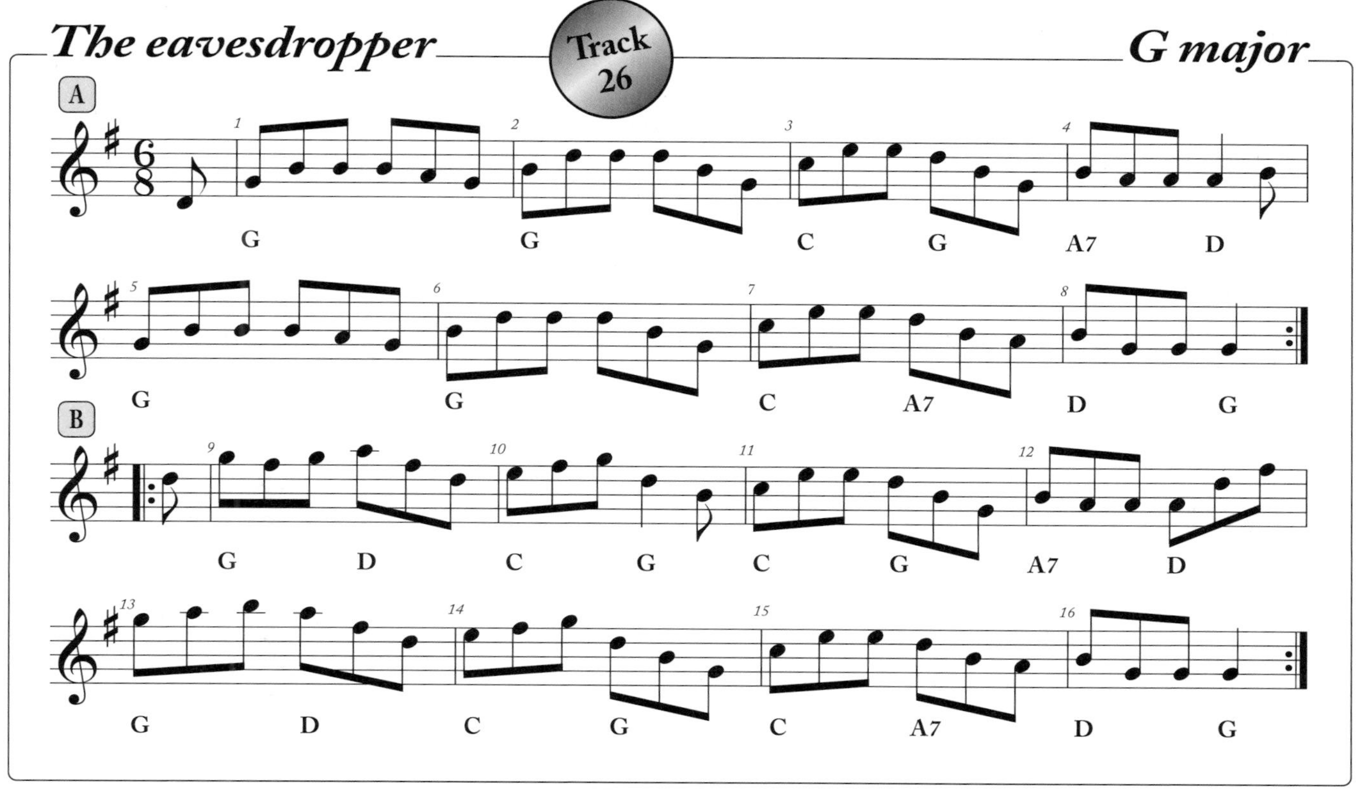

The Cúil Aodha jig — Track 26 — *G major*

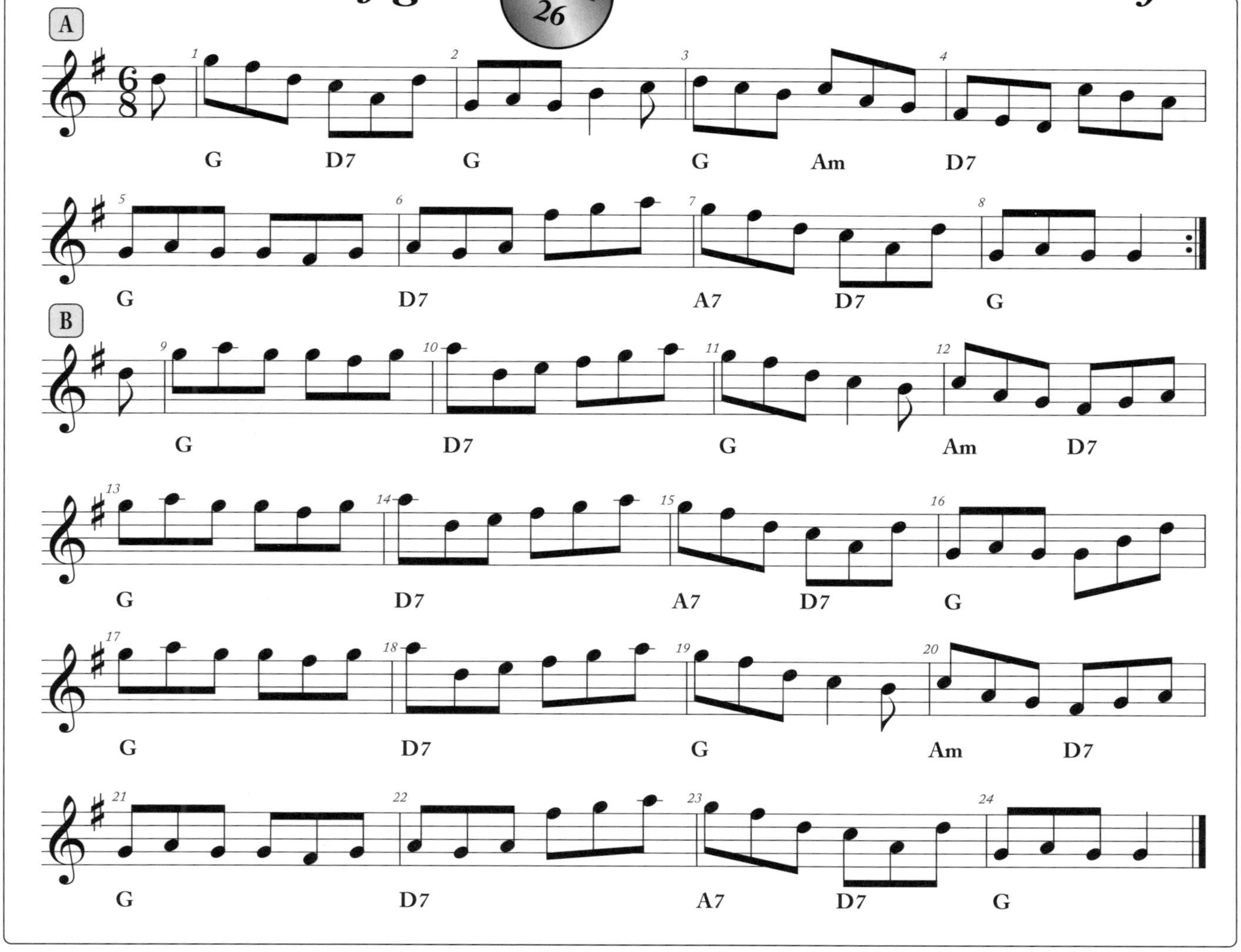
A
G D7 G G Am D7
G D7 A7 D7 G
B
G D7 G Am D7
G D7 A7 D7 G
G D7 G Am D7
G D7 A7 D7 G

The rolling wave — D major

A

D G A7 D D A7

Bm G A7 D G A7

B

D A7 A7 D A7 A7

D A7 Bm F♯m F♯m Em A7

Carman's jig — E minor

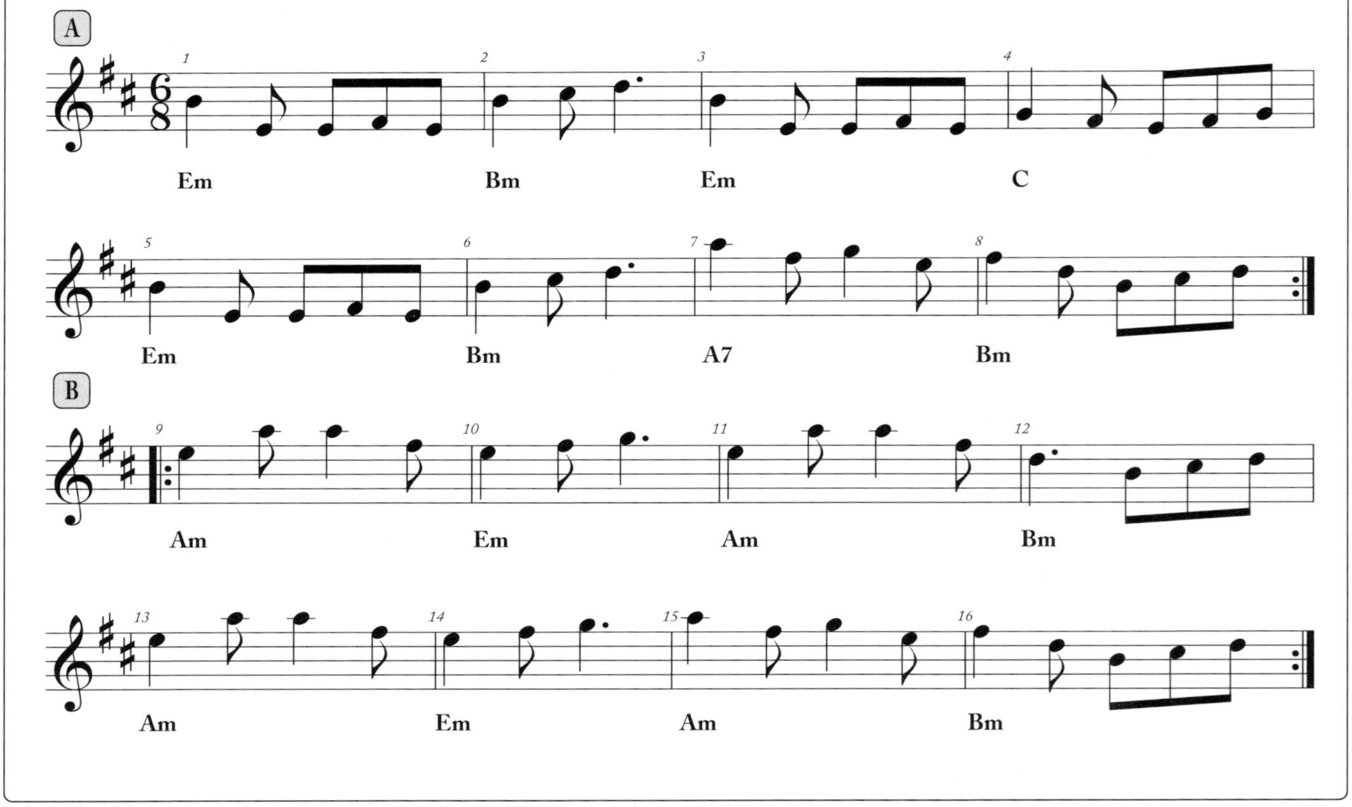

A

Em Bm Em C

Em Bm A7 Bm

B

Am Em Am Bm

Am Em Am Bm

Johnny Leary's slide — *G major*

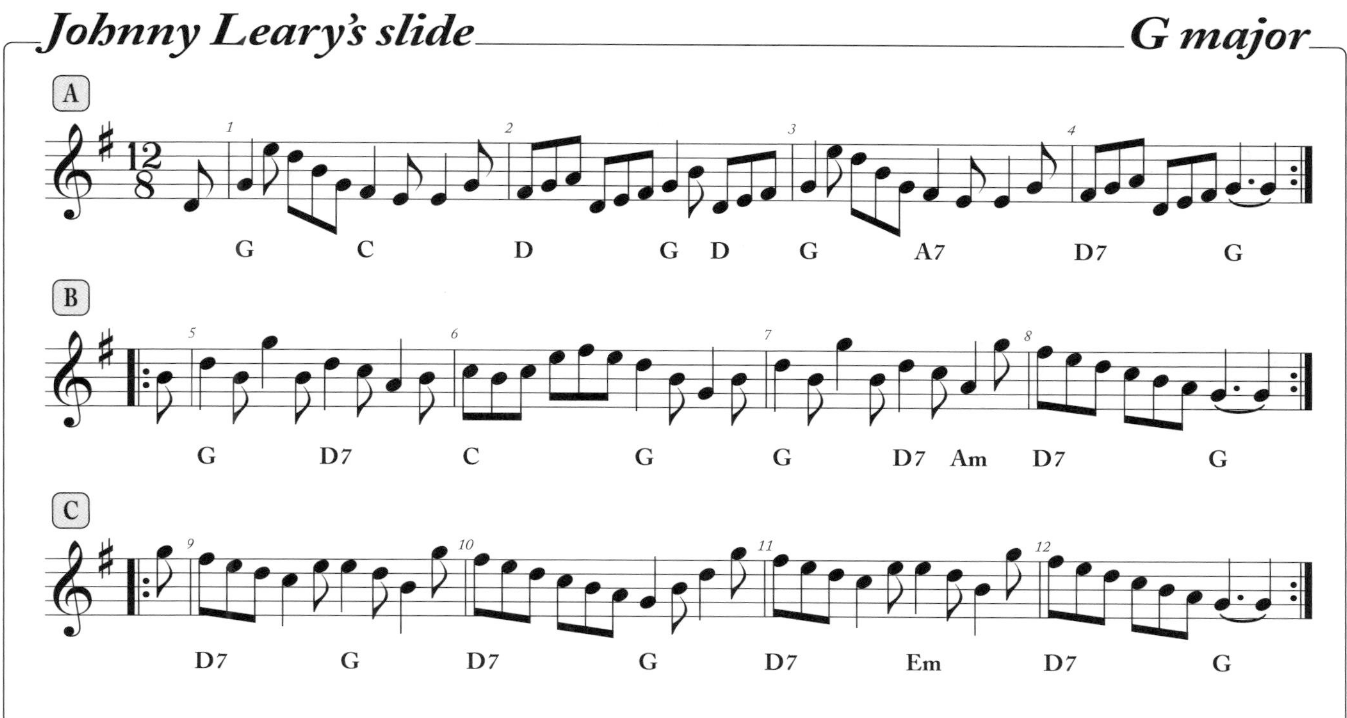

A tune with Gussie Russell, brother of the late Miko and Pakie

A blast at Taffe's pub in Shop Street, Galway City

The flogging

Track 28

G major

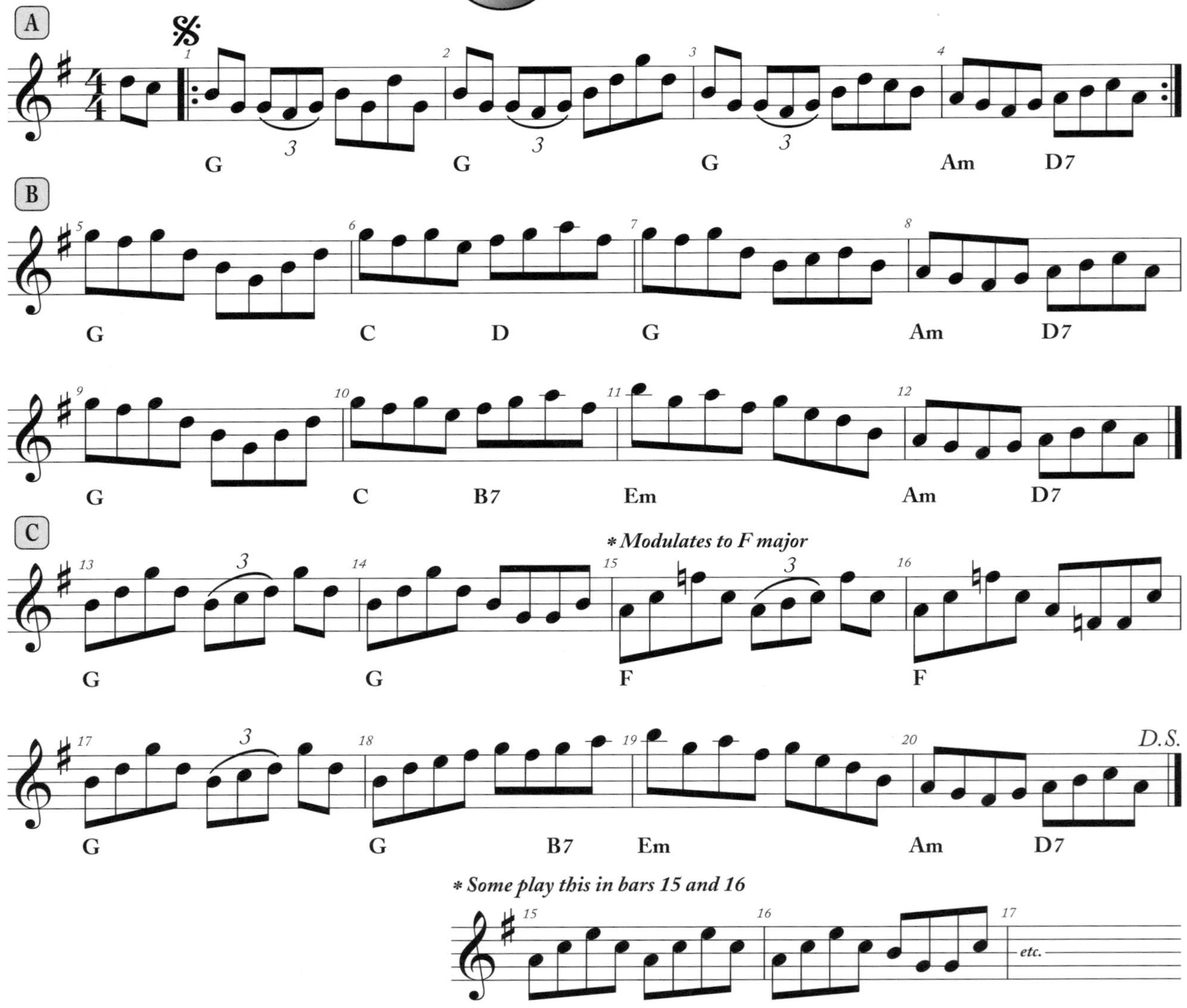

A

G G G Am D7

B

G C D G Am D7

G C B7 Em Am D7

C

** Modulates to F major*

G G F F

D.S.

G G B7 Em Am D7

** Some play this in bars 15 and 16*

etc.

Sailing into Walpole's marsh — Track 28 — *A minor*

A

Am Em Am Em D7

G Em Am Em G Em Am

B

Em Am Em Am Em Am D G

Em Am Em Am C D G

The Dullagen reel — *D major*

A

D G A D G D Em A7

D G A Bm G D A D

B

A D C G A7

D G A Bm G D A D

Christmas eve — G major

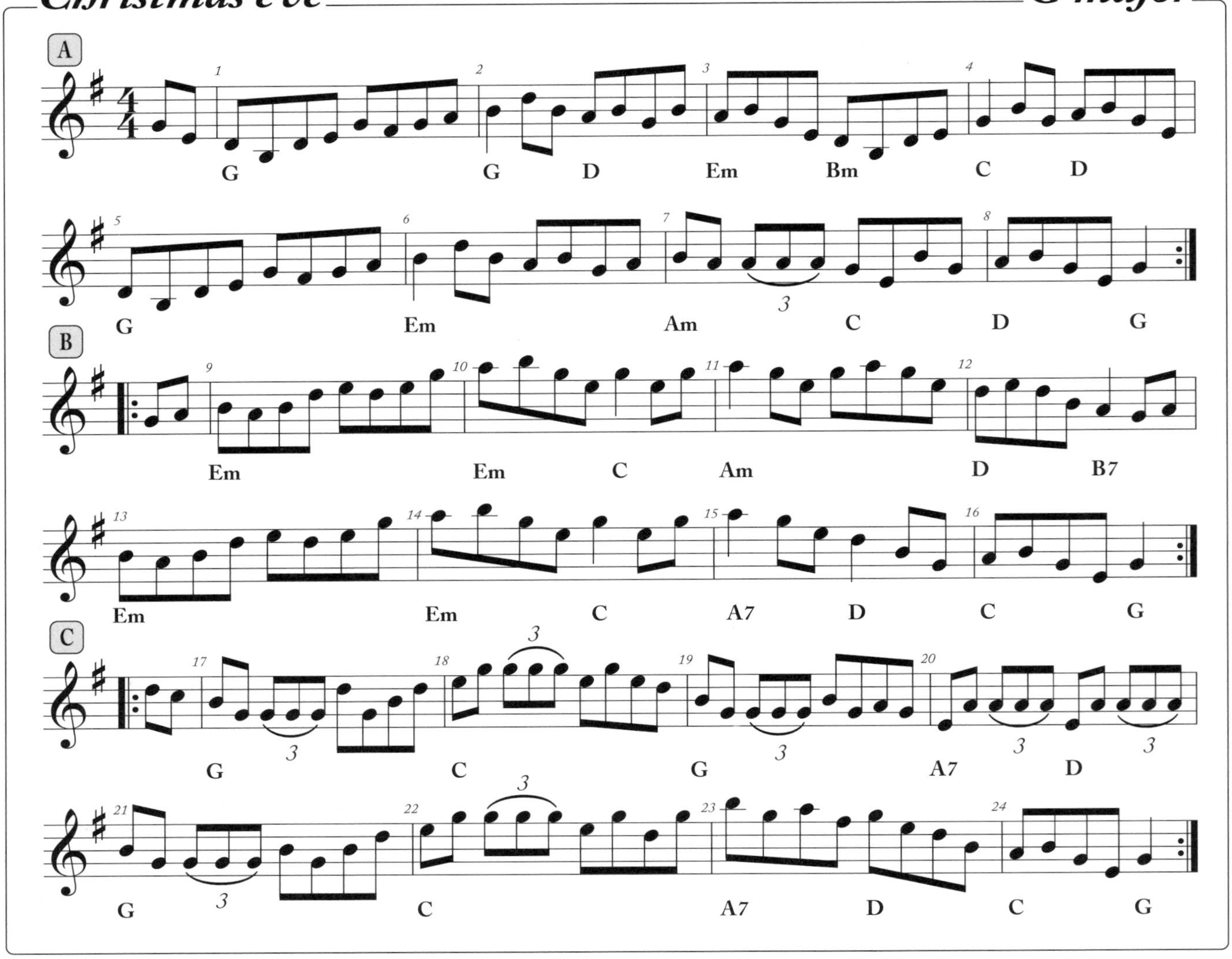
A
G G D Em Bm C D
G Em Am 3 C D G
B
Em Em C Am D B7
Em Em C A7 D C G
C
G 3 C 3 G 3 A7 3 D 3
G 3 C 3 A7 D C G

The Sixmilebridge — D major

Track 29

A
D D A7 D Bm A7 G
B
D G A7 D Bm Em A7 G
D G D A7 D Bm A7 G

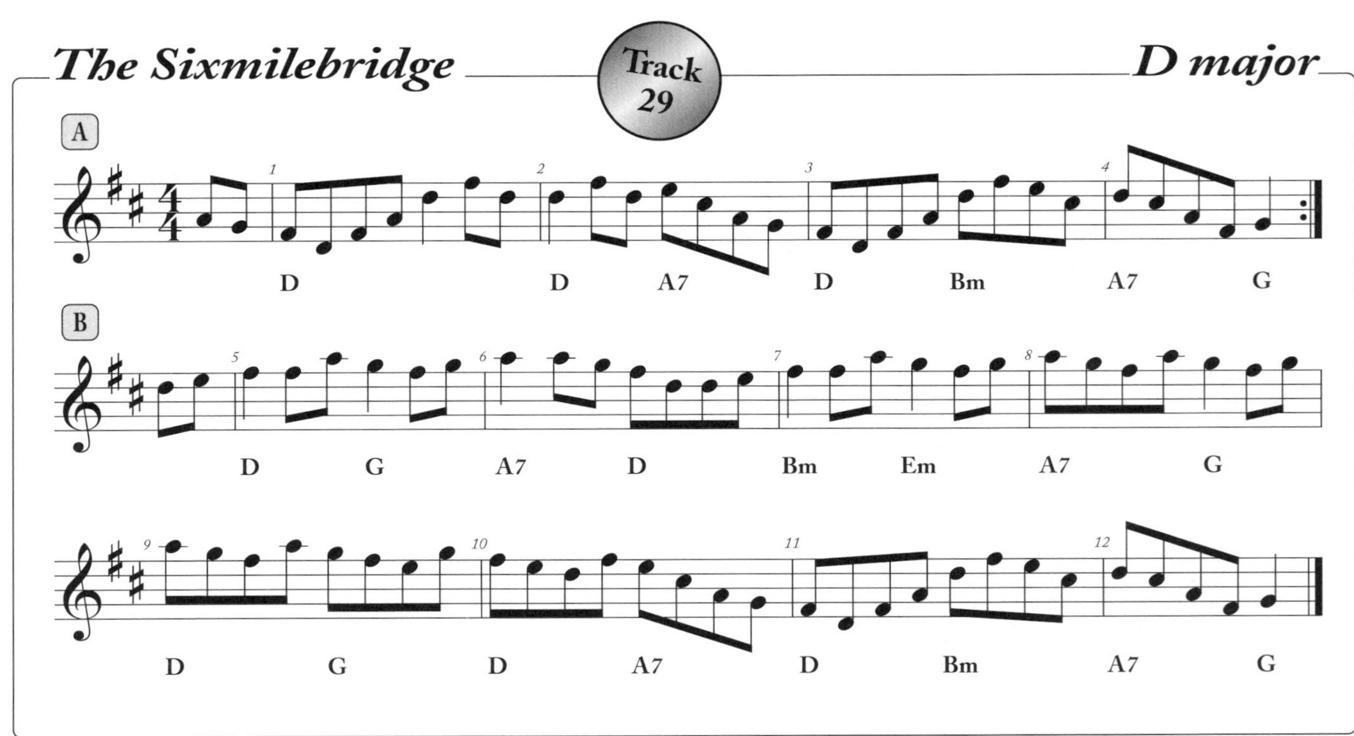

The wheels of the world
Track 29
D modal
A
D C D Bb D
D C D Am C D
B
D C D C D
D C D C A7 D
C D C A7 D
C D A7 A7 D
tr
D.C. al coda
Coda
A7 D A7 D

The glen of Aherlow — *E minor*

A
Em C Bm Em D Em 3
Em C Bm Em D Bm Em 3
B
tr tr tr
Em D Em Bm Em
tr tr
Em D Em C Bm Em

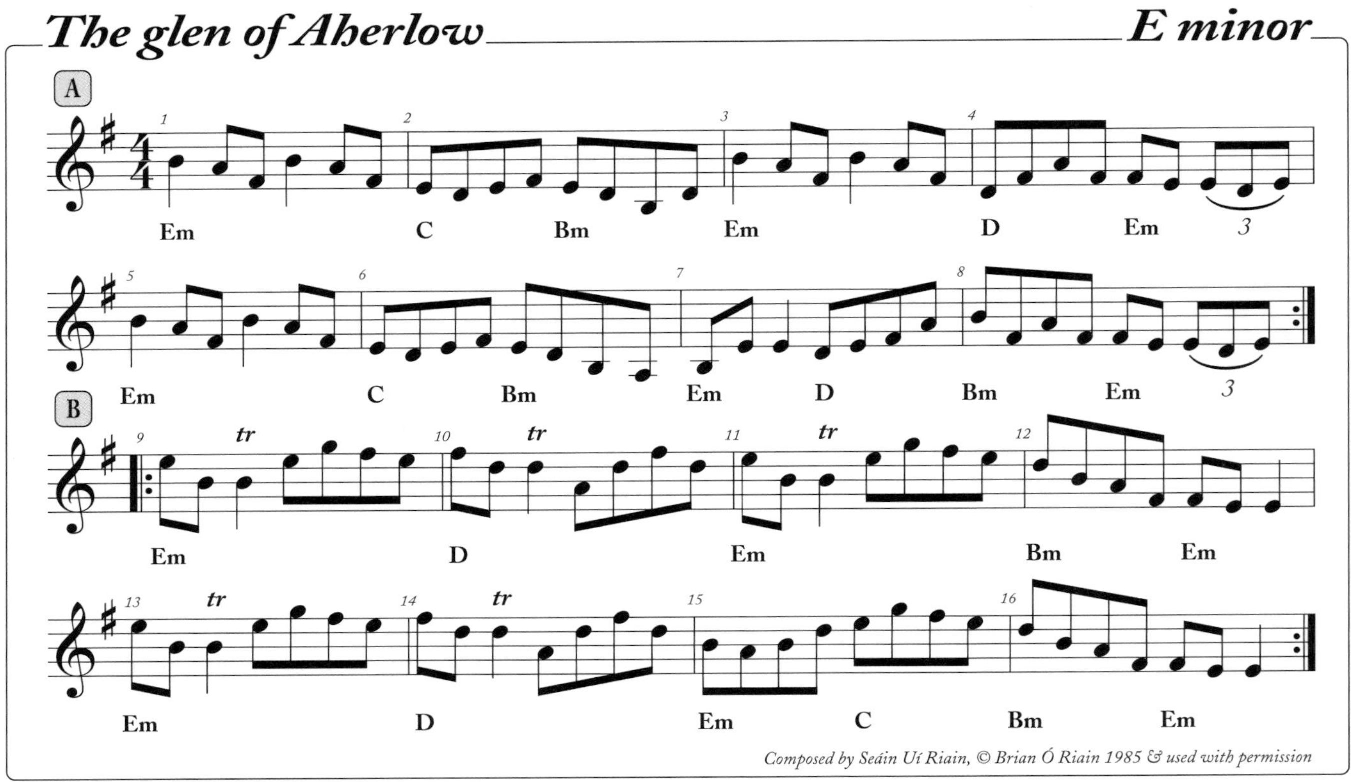

Composed by Seáin Uí Riain, © Brian Ó Riain 1985 & used with permission

Paddy Fahey's no. 1 — *D minor*

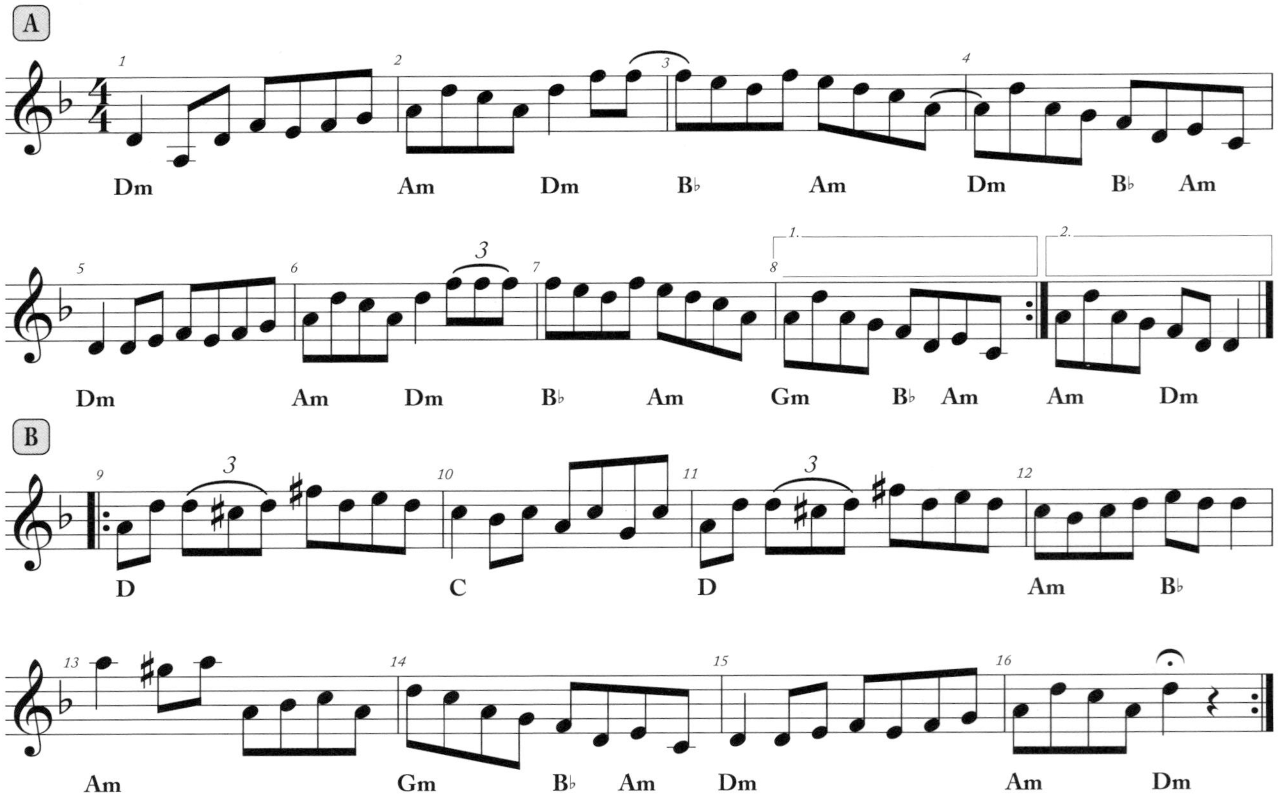
A
Dm Am Dm B♭ Am Dm B♭ Am
1. 2.
Dm Am Dm B♭ Am Gm B♭ Am Am Dm
B
D C D Am B♭
Am Gm B♭ Am Dm Am Dm

The first house in Connaught — G major

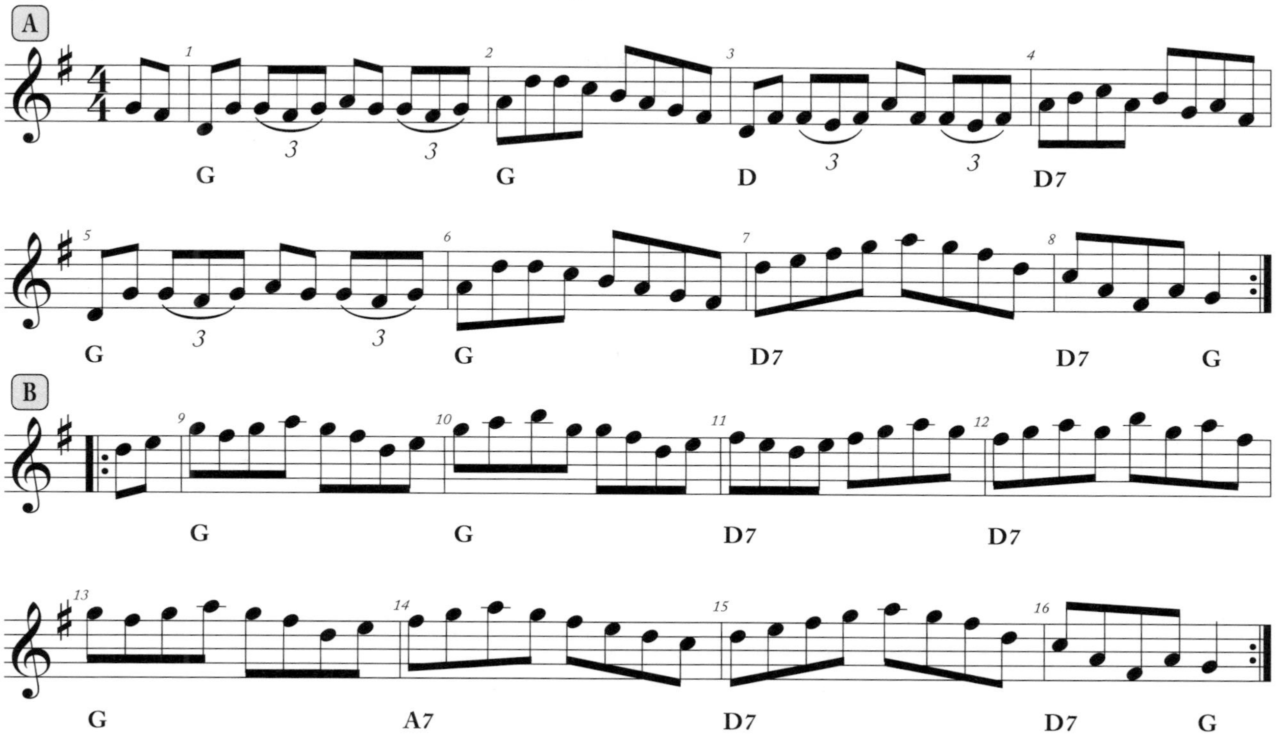

A

G G D D7

G G D7 D7 G

B

G G D7 D7

G A7 D7 D7 G

The steeplechase — D major

A

D Em A7 Bm F♯m G

D Em A7 Bm *tr* A7 D

B

D D A7 D Em A7

D D Em D G A7 D

An páistín fionn

Track 30

E minor

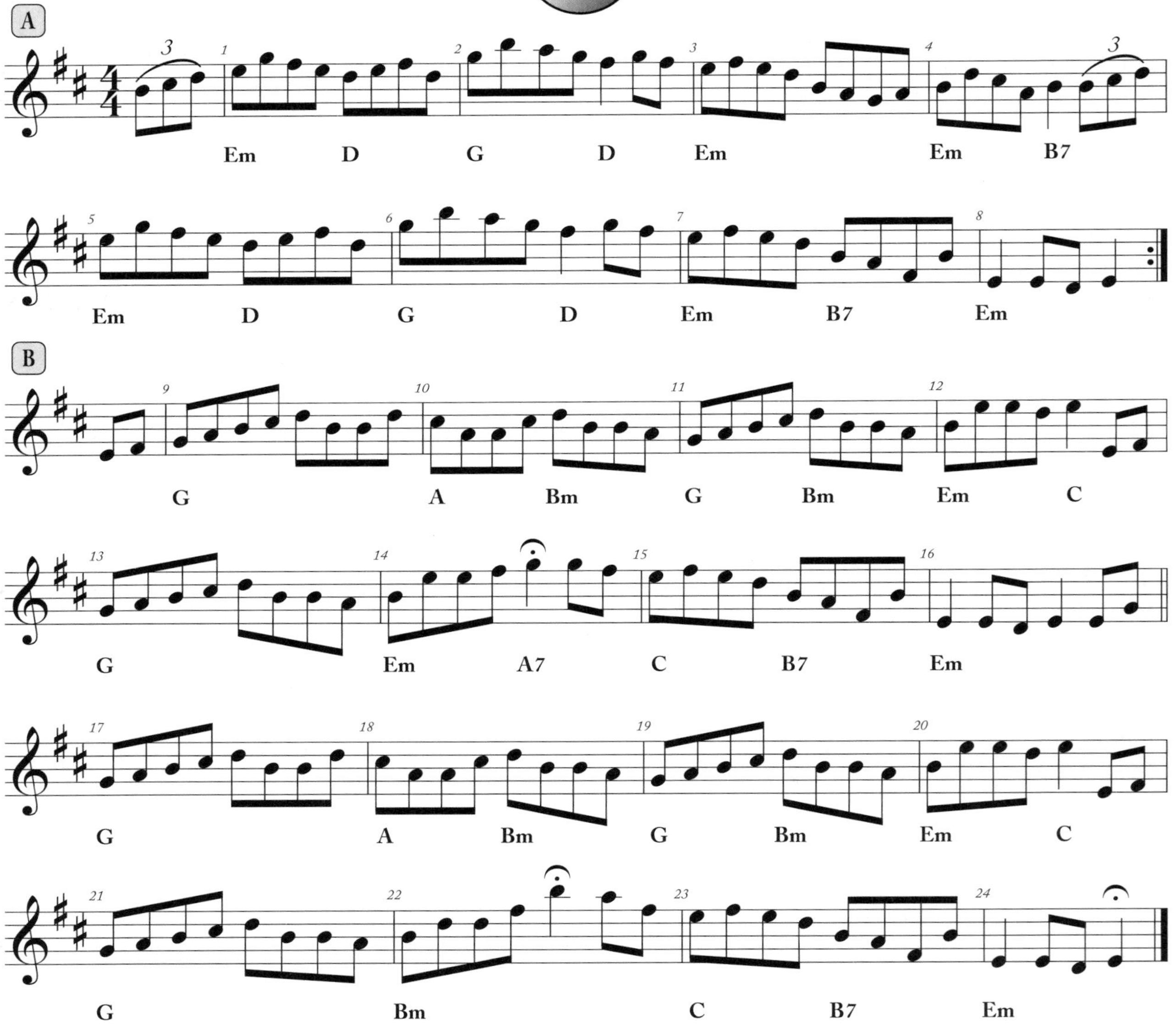

A

Em D G D Em Em B7

Em D G D Em B7 Em

B

G A Bm G Bm Em C

G Em A7 C B7 Em

G A Bm G Bm Em C

G Bm C B7 Em

Daniel O'Connell, the home ruler — *D major*

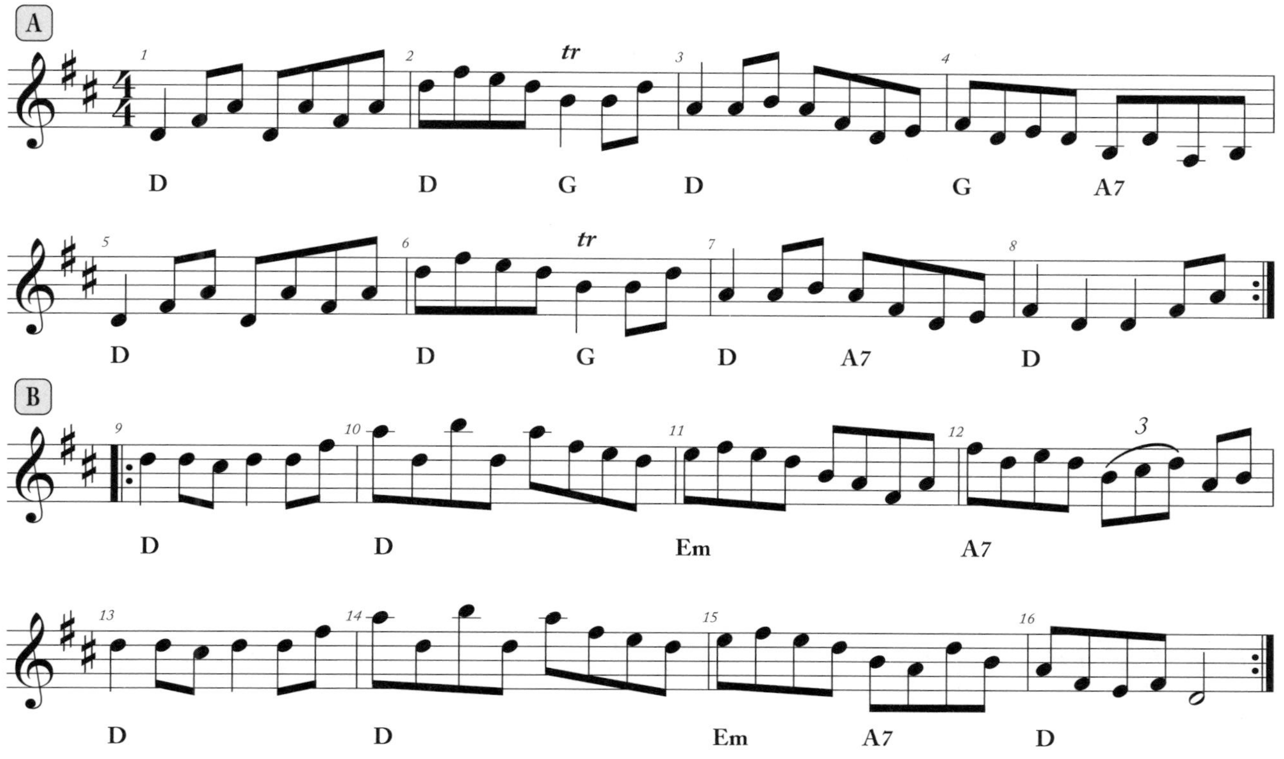
A
tr
D D G D G A7
tr
D D G D A7 D
B
3
D D Em A7
D D Em A7 D

Tomgraney castle — *A minor*

Track 31

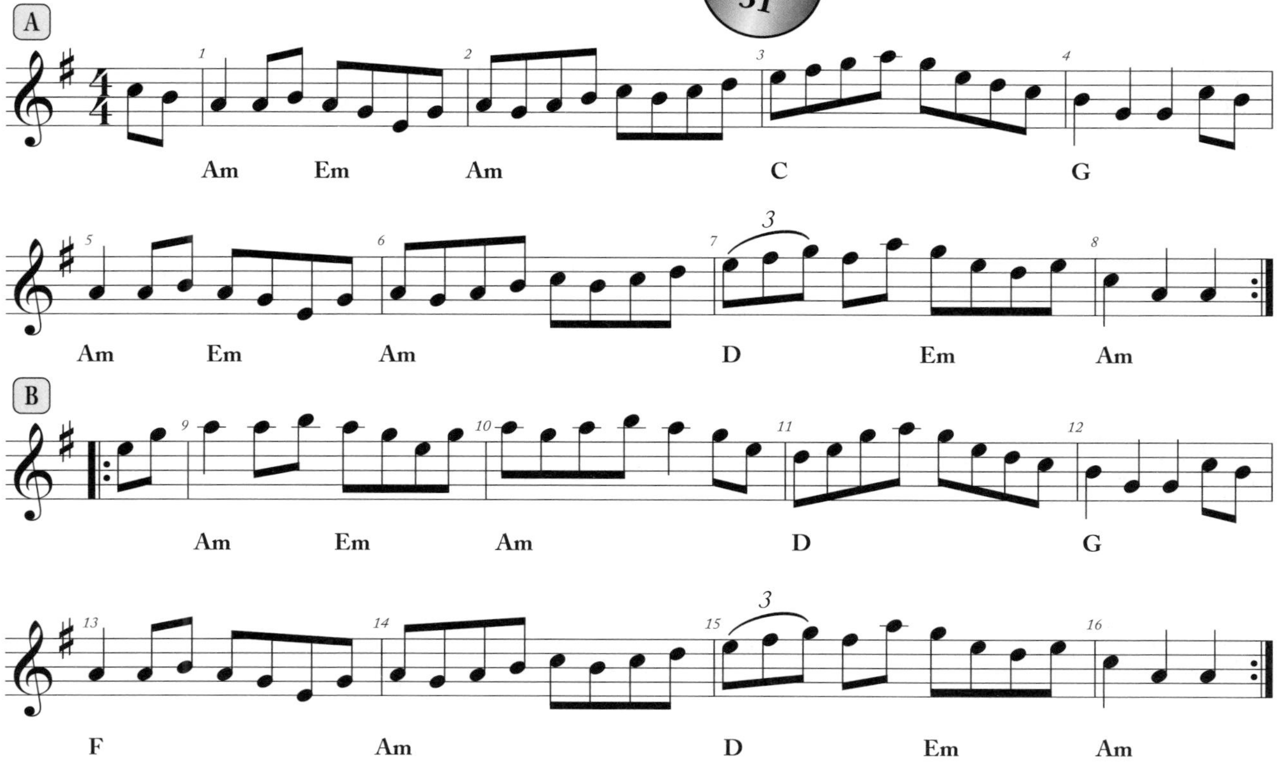
A
Am Em Am C G
3
Am Em Am D Em Am
B
Am Em Am D G
3
F Am D Em Am

The pleasures of home — G minor

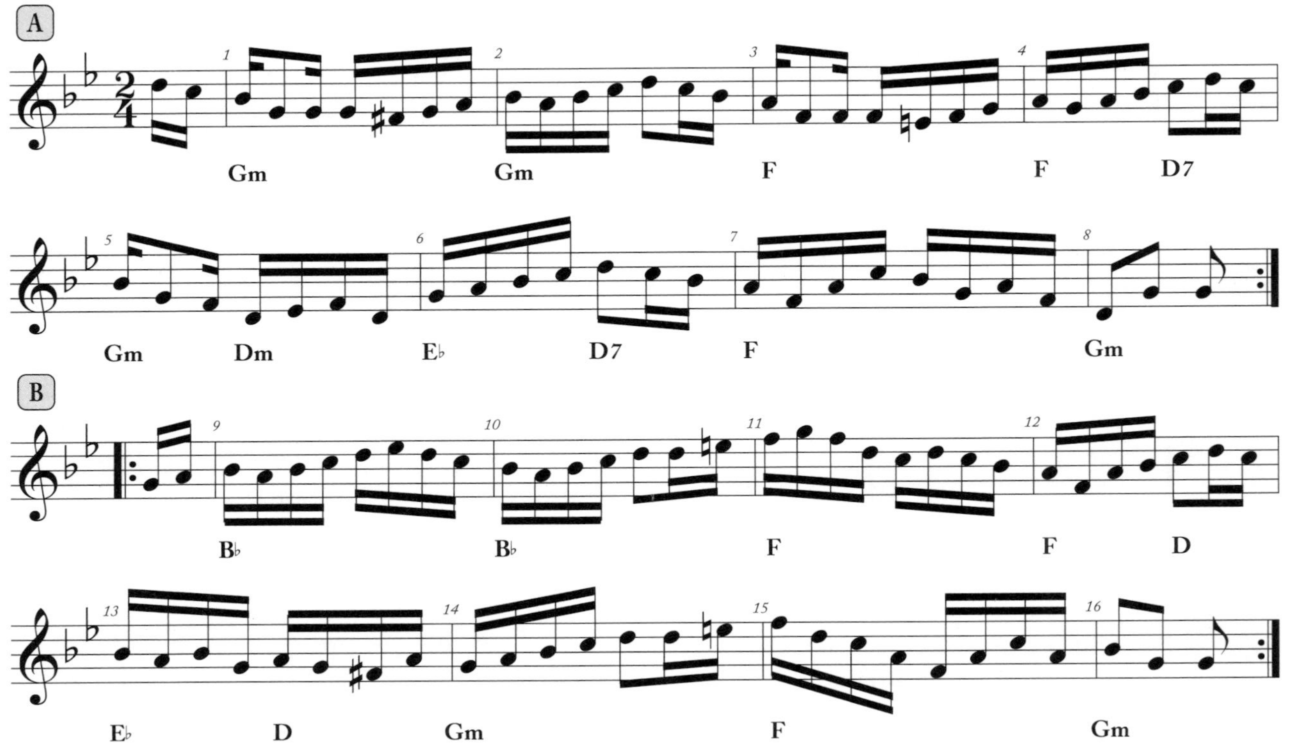

A

Gm Gm F F D7

Gm Dm E♭ D7 F Gm

B

B♭ B♭ F F D

E♭ D Gm F Gm

Mist on the meadow — D minor

A

Dm Am Dm C A7 Dm

Dm Am B♭ Am Dm

B

Am Am Am Am Dm

Am Am D B♭ Am Dm Am Dm

1. 2.

The plains of Boyle — *D major*

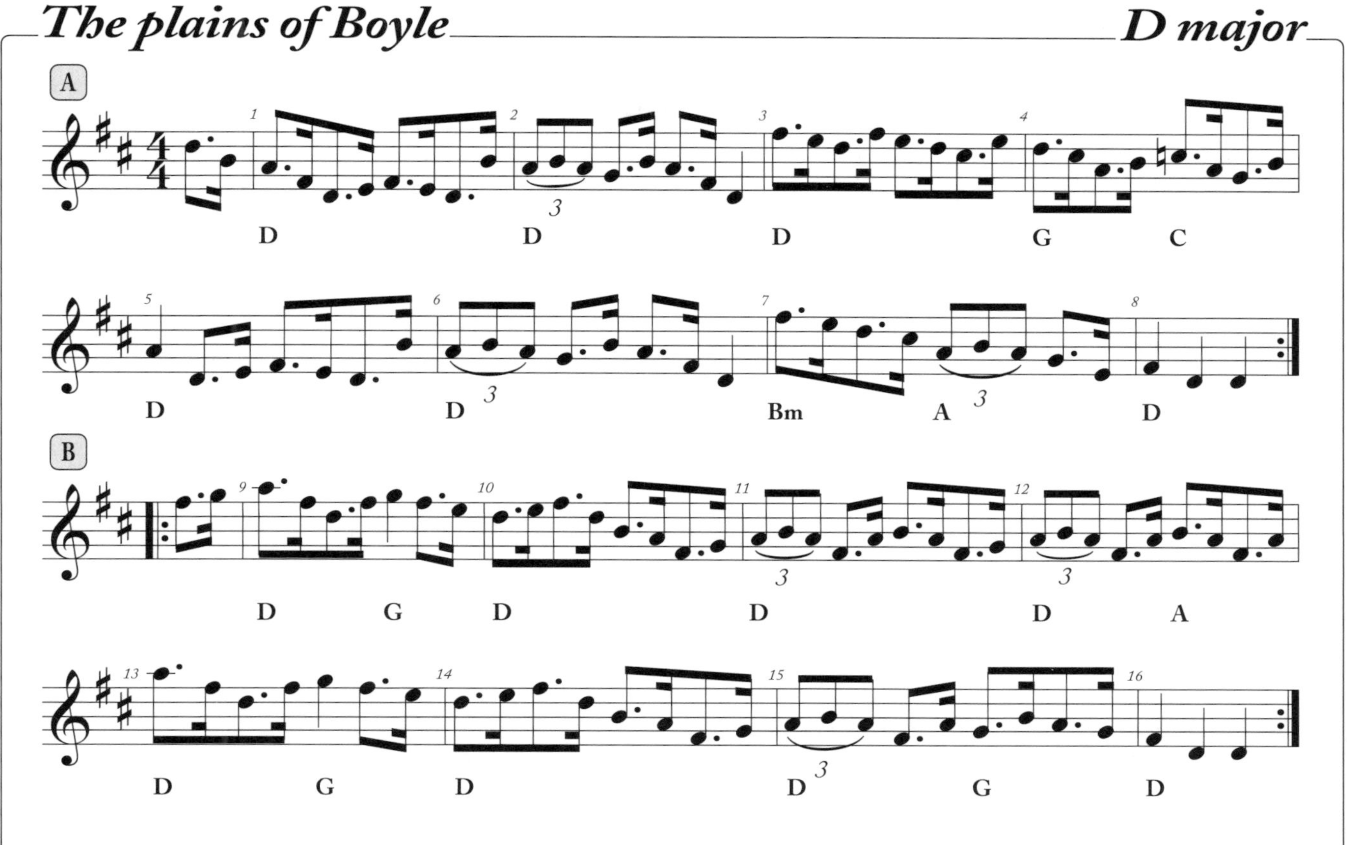

A great music pub in Doolin, County Clare

Linda Bramich

Linda Bramich

Reverting to the other sacred art: guitar and voice in a bar somewhere in Connemara; Jerry Joyce and Anna Lyons are looking on

Peggy Levin — D minor

Princess royal — G minor

O, love, lie beside me — Track 32 — G major

Sullivan O'Moore's march — Track 33 — G major

A

B

C

D

3

I wish my love was in a mire — D major

A

B

Appendix Two

Keys available in other tunings

As you have seen from the tutor, the system has been explained for a concertina tuned in G and C. This does not prevent the method being adopted for any other tuning of concertina that may come your way in time.

Let us look at probably the most common tuning other than G/C, that of D and G. Because of the larger reeds used in these instruments, air control may become a bigger headache but press on; you will see that the range of keys is just as varied.

So, a D/G concertina, using the G method from this tutor, will have you playing in D major. The D method will produce A major; F major will equate to C major and A major becomes E major.

The minor keys will likewise be altered downward by a fourth so that A minor becomes E minor; B minor will play F♯ minor; D minor is now A minor; E minor becomes B minor and G minor moves to D minor. Any given key will be one octave lower than when played on the G/C box.

Modulation is handled in exactly the same way and decoration is there on all instruments for your own invention.

Rather than go through all this again, I will simply list the key of the instrument, the system that applies to G and C Anglos and, after the ⇨ symbol, the transposed key that will be achieved.

The table covers the most likely keys but there are freaky models such as those in E and A. These are extremely rare. In any case, you only need to sharpen by one semitone those keys shown for the E♭/A♭ type to get the possible range.

For a D and G concertina

C major	⇨	**G major**
G major	⇨	**D major**
D major	⇨	**A major**
A major	⇨	**E major**
F major	⇨	**C major**
A minor	⇨	**E minor**
E minor	⇨	**B minor**
D minor	⇨	**A minor**
B minor	⇨	**F sharp minor**
G minor	⇨	**D minor**

For an F and B♭ concertina

C major	⇨	**B♭ major**
G major	⇨	**F major**
D major	⇨	**C major**
A major	⇨	**G major**
F major	⇨	**E♭ major**
A minor	⇨	**G minor**
E minor	⇨	**D minor**
D minor	⇨	**C minor**
B minor	⇨	**A minor**
G minor	⇨	**F minor**

For an E♭ and A♭ concertina

C major	⇨	**A♭ major**
G major	⇨	**E♭ major**
D major	⇨	**B♭ major**
A major	⇨	**F major**
F major	⇨	**D♭ major**
A minor	⇨	**F minor**
E minor	⇨	**C minor**
D minor	⇨	**B♭ minor**
B minor	⇨	**G minor**
G minor	⇨	**E♭ minor**

Appendix Three

Chord patterns

These diagrams give the principal major and minor chords related to the keys described in the tutor. The majority of them are left-hand only.

Left-hand pushed chords

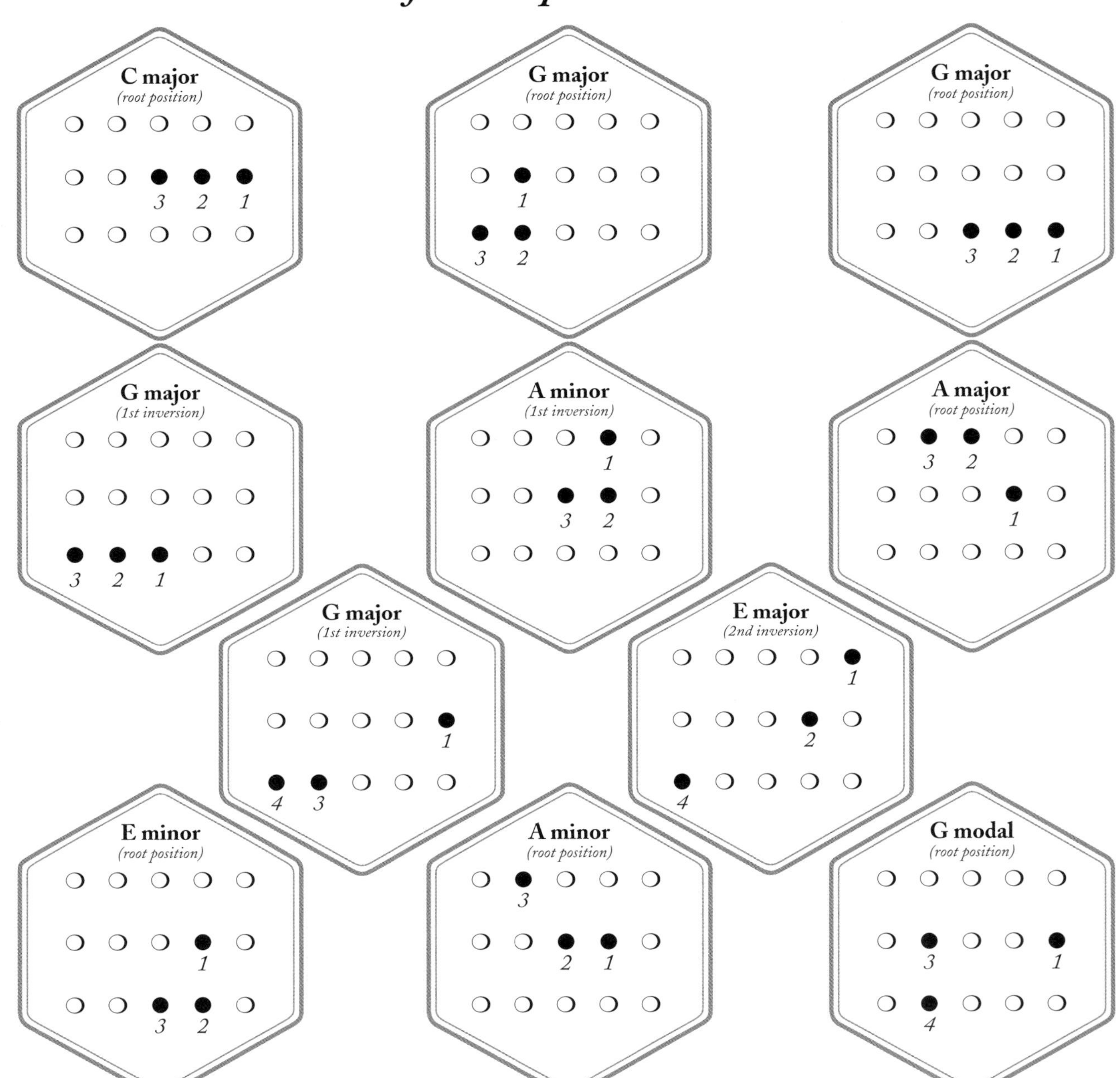

Chord formations

Chord	B♭	F	C	G	D	A	E	B	F♯	Gm	Dm	Am	Em	Bm	F♯m	C7	G7	D7	A7	E7	B7
Root	B♭	F	C	G	D	A	E	B	F♯	G	D	A	E	B	F♯	C	G	D	A	E	B
Third	D	A	E	B	F♯	C♯	G♯	D♯	A♯	B♭	F	C	G	D	A	E	B	F♯	C♯	G♯	D♯
Fifth	F	C	G	D	A	E	B	F♯	C♯	D	A	E	B	F♯	C♯	G	D	A	E	B	F♯
Seventh																B♭	F	C	G	D	A

Left-hand pulled chords

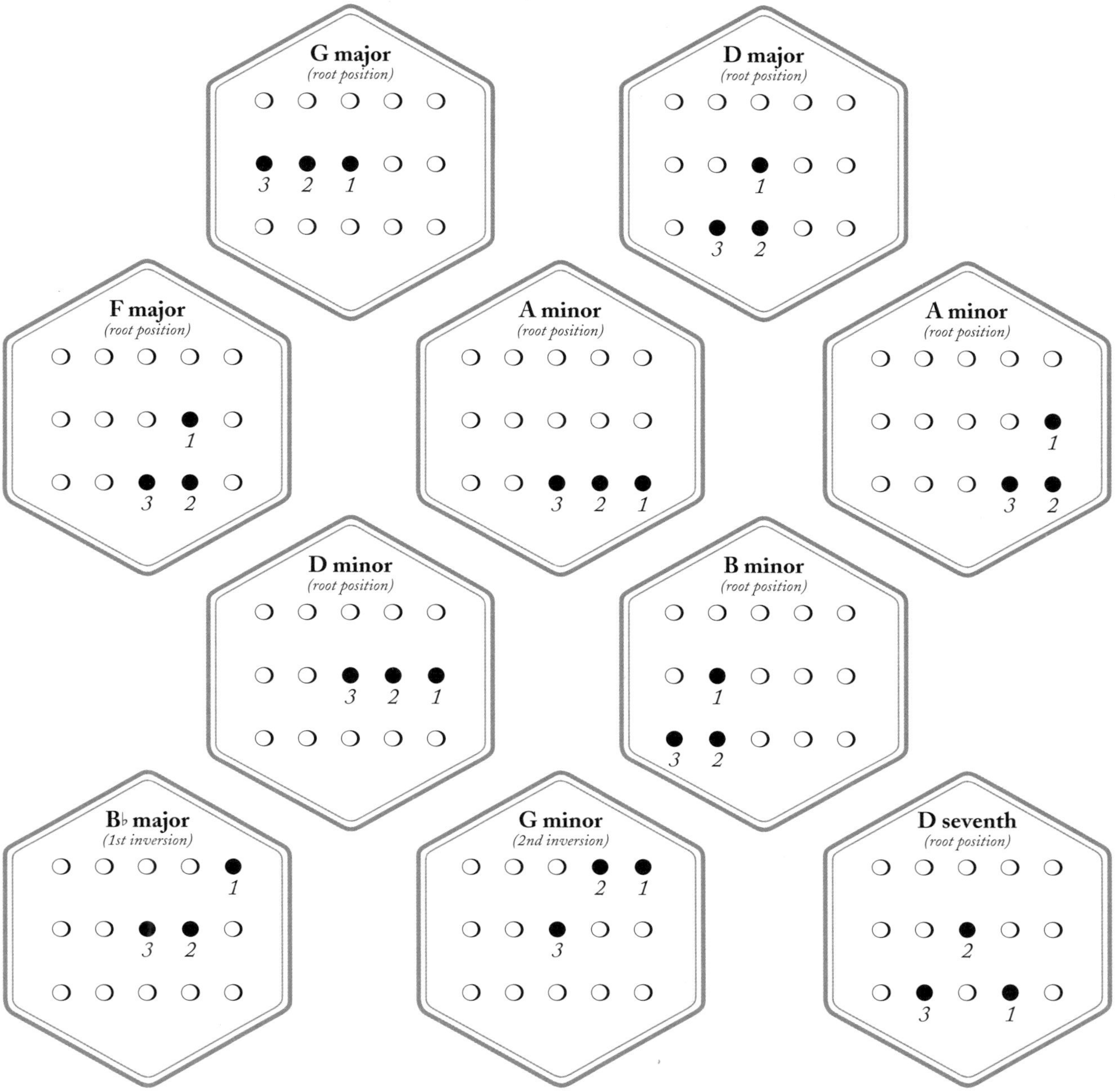

G major
(root position)

D major
(root position)

F major
(root position)

A minor
(root position)

A minor
(root position)

D minor
(root position)

B minor
(root position)

B♭ major
(1st inversion)

G minor
(2nd inversion)

D seventh
(root position)

Left- and right-hand pulled chords

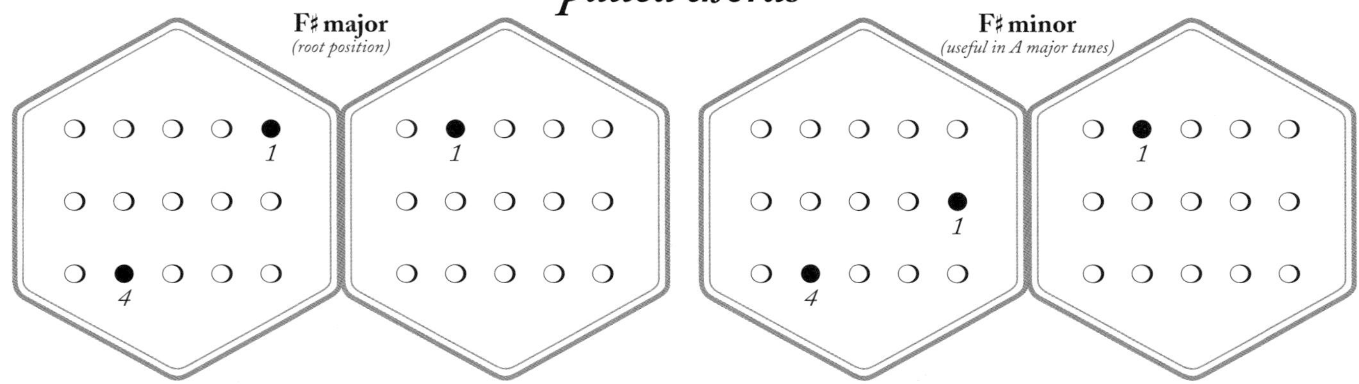

Appendix Four

Rudiments of music

Chromatic scale

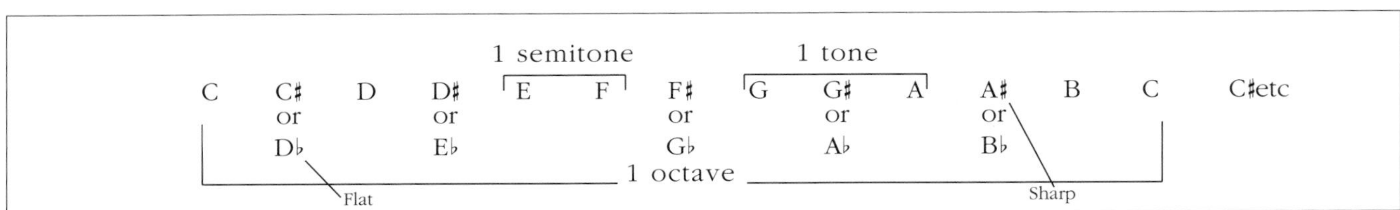

Treble clef

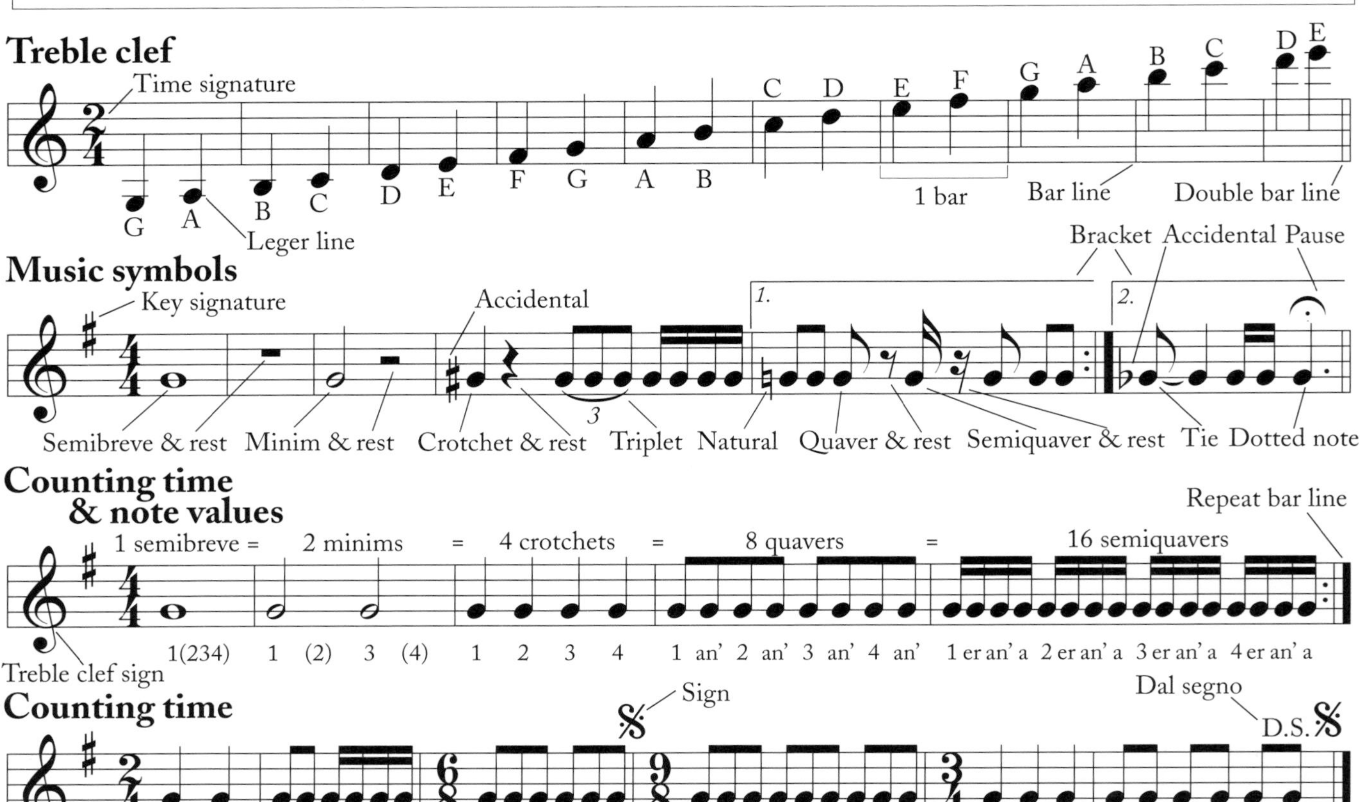

Glossary

Accidental — is a note which is altered to *sharp, flat* or *natural* and is foreign to the key indicated by the key signature. An accidental sign applies to the note it precedes and, unless contradicted, all further notes of that pitch up to the end of the bar.

Bracket — play the bar under '1' the first time through; substitute the bar under '2' on the repeat.

Chromatic scale — consists entirely of semitones.

Dal segno — return to the sign and repeat.

Diatonic scale — consists of a series of notes from the chromatic scale at set intervals, e.g. the major scale (do-re-me etc) has intervals of: *tone, tone, semitone, tone tone, tone, semitone.* Thus the scale of C is *C, D, E, F, G, A, B, C* and the scale of D is *D, E, F♯, G, A, B C♯, D.* Tunes take all or most of their notes from a particular diatonic scale. Each scale has its own set number of sharps or flats.

Dotted note — a dot placed after a note lengthens that note by half. Thus ♩. = ♩‿♪

Double bar line — marks the end of an individual section or part of a tune. A 'final' bar line can indicate the end of a piece or the end of a principal section. A final bar line preceded by two dots indicates that that particular section has to be repeated.

Fine — (pronounced 'feenay') means end.

Key signature — shows which notes have to be sharpened or flattened. It also gives an indication of the key. Keys are named by the first note of the scale.

Rest — denotes a period of silence, of specified length.

Tie — joins two notes of the same pitch and denotes a single sustained note with a time value of the two combined.

Time signature — resembles a fraction. The top number indicates the number of beats per bar; the bottom number indicates the time unit for the beat (2 = a minim, 4 = a crotchet, 8 = a quaver, 16 = a semiquaver). For example, $\frac{4}{4}$ = 4 beats per bar occurring every crotchet.

Triplet — consists of three notes played in the time of two of the same value.

Appendix five

Dealers and suppliers

Barleycorn Concertinas
67 Little Chell Lane
Tunstall
Stoke-on-Trent
Staffordshire
England
ST6 6LZ
Telephone 01782 816504

Oundle Music
13 West Street
Oundle
Peterborough
Cambridgeshire
England
PE8 4ET
Telephone 01832 73669

Marcus Music
Tredegar House
Newport
Gwent
Wales
NP1 9YW
Telephone 01633 815612

The Button Box
9 East Pleasant Street
Amherst
MA 01002
U.S.A.
Telephone 00 1 413 549 0171

Hobgoblin Music
17 Northgate Parade
Crawley
West Sussex
England
RH10 2DT
Telephone 01293 515858

The Music Room
35 Bradford Road
Cleckheaton
West Yorkshire
England
BD19 3JN
Telephone 01274 879768

All the above, if trading by the time you read this, deal in second-hand instruments. Hobgoblin Music also sell new concertinas from ex-Crabb maker Connor, from C. Wheatstone & Co and, for the budget-minded, from Bastari (often under the name of Gremlin).

The availability of new instruments depends upon what is in stock. You can wait for a year or more to get a specific model made to your requirements. If you *are* prepared to wait, then I can recommend no better source for information about quality makers than the magazine *Concertina and Squeezebox*, edited by Joel Cowan and available from him in America or in the British Isles from that concertina maker of outstanding reputation, Colin Dipper. Their addresses are as follows:

Colin Dipper
West End House
High Street, Heytesbury
Warminster
Wiltshire
England
BA12 0EA
Telephone 01985 40516

Joel Cowan
PO box 6706
Ithaca
New York
14851
U.S.A.
Telephone 00 1 607 273 2440
Facsimile 607 277 0801

Appendix six

Bibliography

There are many more books of tunes on the market but the following come highly recommended and will provide you with a wide range of challenges and more tunes than you'll ever have time to learn! Visiting music stalls at folk festivals throughout these islands will reward you with the chance to trawl through a treasury of printed traditional music, more often than not sold by people who can talk knowledgeably about their wares. If you want to get into the folk festival scene then several 'folk festival guides' now appear during March and April and are a must. The best source of printed and recorded traditional music via mail order is rightly recognised as being that belonging to the publishers of the work you are holding.

100 Essential Irish Session Tunes
Edited Dave Mallinson, *published mally productions, ISBN 1 899512 18 7*
Arguably the most widely-played and -known jigs and reels to help ease you into a session: with a selection of these tunes, you can be confident someone in the session will join in. With chords.

100 Enduring Irish Session Tunes
Edited Dave Mallinson, *published mally productions, ISBN 1 899512 19 5*
Broader in emphasis and away from reels (though still containing some) than the above, this selection of 'session-friendly' tunes forms part of the basic repertoire of a player of Irish music. With chords.

The Anglo Concertina De-Mystified
Written Bertram Levy, *published Front Hall Enterprises, Inc*
11 lessons, the first few of which are suitable for the 20-button machine.

Ceol Rince na hÉireann, cuid 1, 2, 3, 4 agus 5
Edited Breandán Breathnach, *published An Gúm*
Three volumes containing individual versions of jigs, reels, hornpipes, polkas and slides compiled by a highly-respected scholar of the genre; vital for all serious musicians.

The Crossroads Dance
Published mally productions, ISBN 1 899512 10 1
All the tunes from two recordings of céilí band *Shaskeen,* with chords and copious footnotes concerning the tunes.

The Dance Music of Ireland: 1,001 Gems
Edited Captain Francis O'Neill, *published Walton's Manufacturing Ltd*
A facsimile of O'Neill's most influential work. It is a revision and improvement of his earlier book of 1,850 melodies and the more useful of the two, albeit extremely dated.

The Darley and McCall Collection of Traditional Irish Music
Edited Arthur Darley and Patrick McCall, *published Ossian Publications, ISBN 0 946005 23 0*
Interesting mainly from the historical standpoint, particularly as regards the editors' notes about the tunes, but this book does actually contain one or two jewels.

The Fiddler's Tune-Book
Edited Peter Kennedy, *published mally productions, ISBN 1 899512 14 4*
Staple fare for many a musician since the early 1950s. Any collection of traditional music from the British Isles will, undoubtedly, contain some Irish tunes due to the constant interchange that has existed between the four nations since the earliest times, hence the inclusion of this possibly misnamed volume in a concertina tutor's bibliography. English folk song is also indebted to the thousands of Irish labourers who built the canals and railways and gave their airs to the native working class to utilise in their own ongoing traditions. With chords.

The Golden Eagle
Edited Donncha Ó Briain, *published Comhaltas Ceoltóirí Éireann*
Plenty of standards in this one, giving an overview of one Irish musician's and teacher's very traditional repertoire.

The Hidden Ireland, The First Selection of Irish Traditional Compositions of Sheáin Uí Riain

Edited Brian Ó Riain, *published Brian Ó Riain, ISBN 0 9513415 0 2*

Seán Ryan was one of the unsung heroes of Irish music. Many of his compositions are taken as traditional, such as *The Reel of Rio, The Castle Jig* (in A minor and *Seán Ryan's* in popular parlance) plus the one in this tutor, *The Glen of Aherlow.*

The Irish Fiddle Book

Written Matt Cranitch, *published Mercier Press ISBN 0 85342 803 4*

The inclusion of a fiddle tutor may be seen as odd listed in a concertina tutor but never judge a book by its cover. Not only does it contain 101 clearly written tunes, including some slow airs, but it also deals comprehensively with ornamentation from, obviously, a different viewpoint. Also, the recordings of the tunes are in concert pitch and at a manageable speed.

Irish Tin Whistle Legends

Edited Tommy Walsh, *published Walton's Manufacturing Ltd*

A great source of Irish dance tunes of all types.

An Irish Tunebook, parts 1 **and** 2

Edited John Loesberg, *published Ossian Publications, ISBN 0 946005 31 1 and 0 946005 32 X*

An eclectic selection of tune types featuring several airs and song tunes.

Karen Tweed's Irish Choice

Edited Karen Tweed, *published mally productions, ISBN 1 899512 12 8*

Karen's accordion sounds almost concertina-like! She chose these tunes to represent her favourites without excluding many more familiar selections. The recordings available to match the book are an inspiration to players of any instrument. With chords.

Music For The Sets

Published mally productions, ISBN (The Yellow Book) 1 899512 32 2, (The Blue Book) 1 899512 33 0

All of the tunes from six absolutely cracking recordings of set dance music. These two compilations have a unique character: they are representative of both tunes needed for the dance *and* personal preferences of some top traditional musicians. With chords.

Music of Ireland

Published mally productions, ISBN (Where's the Crack?) 1 899512 27 6, (A Mighty Tune!) 1 899512 28 4, (The Big Session…) 1 899512 29 2, (Give Us Another) 1 899512 30 6, (Fire Away, Now!!) 1 899512 31 4

Tunes collected from the sessions around the British Isles, around seventy per book; each compilation has its own 'personality'. With chords.

The Roche Collection of Traditional Irish Music

Edited Frank Roche, *published Ossian Publications, ISBN 0 946005 05 2*

An under-rated book, containing 566 airs, marches and dance tunes.

Through the Half-Door

Published mally productions, ISBN 1 899512 09 8

Notated from three recordings of céilí band *Shaskeen,* with copious footnotes concerning the tunes and plenty of encouragement to look further. With chords.

Traditional Irish Tin Whistle Tutor

Edited Geraldine Cotter, *published Ossian Publications, ISBN 0 946005 12 5*

The same comments apply here as apply to The Irish Fiddle Book; this book also contains a healthy selection of tunes and slow airs. Plus, if the concertina *does* turn out to beat you…

Traditional Slow Airs of Ireland

Edited Tomás Ó Canainn, *published Ossian Publications, ISBN 0 946005 84 2*

118 airs compiled by a scholar of the music; this book is virtually a milestone in the documentation of Irish music.

Appendix seven

Discography

Terry Bingham:
'Terry Bingham' *own label* TB001

Terry Bingham, John Kelly, Tommy McMahon and **Bernard O'Sullivan** plus various other artistes:
'Farewell To Lissycasey' *Ossian* OSS79

Jack and **Father Charlie Coen:**
'The Branch Line' *Green Linnet* GL3067

Elizabeth Crotty:
'Concertina Music from West Clare' *RTÉ* RTÉ225

Cathy Custy:
'An Ceoltoir Fánach' *own label*

Jackie Daly:
'Jackie Daly' *Ossian* OSS30

Chris Droney:
'The Fertile Rock' *Cló Iar-Chonnachta* CI110

Chris Droney:
'Irish Dance Music' *Copley* COP5007

Noel Hill, Tony Mac Mahon and Iarla Ó Lionáird:
'Aislingí Ceoil (Music Of Dreams)' *Gael-Linn* CEF164

Noel Hill and Tony Mac Mahon:
'I gCnoc na Graí' *Gael-Linn* CEF114

Noel Hill:
'The Irish Concertina' *Claddagh* CCF21

Tommy Keane and Jaqueline McCarty with Alec Finn:
'The Wind Among the Reeds' *Maree Music Co* MMC51

Gabriel McArdle, Ben Lennon, Séamus Quinn and Ciarán Curran:
'Dog Big And Dog Little' *Claddagh* 4CC51

Jacqueline McCarthy:
'The Hidden Note' *Maree Music Co* MMC53

Tommy McCarthy:
'Sporting Nell' *Maree Music Co* MMC52

John McMahon, Seámus McMahon, Dermot Lernihan, Noreen O'Donaghue, Frank Cullen and Maurice Coyle (collectively 'Fisherstreet'):
'Out In The Night' *Mulligan,* CLUN0057

Mary MacNamara:
'Traditional Music From East Clare' *Claddagh* 4CC60

William Mullaly:
'The First Irish Concertina Player To Record' *Viva Voce* 005

Bernard O'Sullivan and **Tommy McMahon**:
'Clare Concertinas' *Green Linnet* GL3092

Miko, Gussie and **Pakie Russell**:
'The Russell Family Of Doolin, County Clare' *Ossian* OSS08

Chris Sherburn and Denny Bartley:
'Last Night's Fun!' *Sound Out Music* SOM002

Chris Sherburn and Denny Bartley with Jane Sherburn:
'Foothold' *Sound Out Music* SOM003

Niall Vallely, Liz Doherty, Gerry McKee, Frank Torpey and John Spillane (collectively 'Nomos'):
'I Won't Be Afraid Any More' *Grapevine* GRA205

John Williams:
'John Williams' *Green Linnet* GL1157

All the above recordings either entirely consist of, or contain a significant amount of, concertina work. The concertina player on each recording is shown in **bold** type. The list is not comprehensive although there is actually not that much concertina music recorded which displays the method demonstrated in this book. Many recordings issued by Comhaltas Ceoltóirí Éireann (The Irish Musician's Association or CCÉ) feature the concertina and some are well worth seeking out by visiting their premises in Dublin. Any album by the group 'Buttons and Bows' (not to be confused with the English album title of the same name) which features Jackie Daly will include some concertina.

A visit to the record stalls at many of the folk festivals in England will prove worthwhile as apart from specialist mail order outlets and, possibly, the dealers mentioned in *Appendix five,* there is virtually nowhere else to browse through more than a handful of titles. Most record shops in England sell nothing of interest to the type of person likely to be reading this except for, perhaps, the current 'hits' of the traditional scene. For mail order, try looking in the specialist 'folk' and 'traditional' press.